"Whatever can go wrong, will

A History of Murphy's Law

by: Nick T. Spark

Originally published as "*The Fastest Man on Earth: A History of Murphy's Law Or Why Everything You Know About Murphy's Law is Wrong*" in the *Annals of Improbable Research* Sept. 2003 and reprinted with permission.

Photographs courtesy of the United States Air Force, David Hill Collection, Author's Collection and as noted.

Special Thanks to Marc Abrahams for his insights and assistance.

Dedicated to:
David Hill Sr., Edward Murphy, George Nichols, Col. John Paul Stapp, the Project MX981 test team, and everyone who ever wondered...

For more information visit: www.historyofmurphyslaw.com

FOREWORD by Marc Abrahams
Annals of Improbable Research

ISBN 0-9786388-9-1

FOREWORD

The history of how Murphy's Law got its name is curiously Murphyesque. Were it not for Nick Spark's good-natured, yet ferociously dogged pursuit of this history, the world would be a slightly dimmer place. We would lack a good, deep look at this absurd beauty of a tale.

Read it, and you'll appreciate the beautiful absurdity of any attempt to track down the real details of any historical incident. The film "Rashomon" has its true-life equivalent here.

And in the reading you will, I hope, appreciate the deep beauty and importance and benefit of that absurd thing, Murphy's Law. Though seemingly undignified, Murphy's Law is a golden law of engineering, planning and organizing. Attend closely to what the protagonists here say about The Law. Hear the reverence in their voices when they speak of it, as well as the low chuckling.

"Nick Spark" is a perfect name for a technology-adventure-hero but, as far as I'm aware, Nick T. Spark, the author, really does bear that name. In May 2003, I received an email message from Nick, then a stranger to me. He said he was working on a history of Murphy's Law, and asked if my magazine, the "Annals of Improbable Research", might like to publish it. The article, when it arrived, was much longer than what we usually run. Despite that it seemed just about perfect: It makes the reader laugh and then think. We were and are honored and proud to have published it.

Almost everyone has heard of Murphy's Law, but few know more than the jokey phrase "Whatever can go wrong, will." The individuals who were involved with the birth and subsequent history of the phrase "Murphy's Law" each know a particular slice, big or small, of the story. But try to put any two of those slices together and you'll see that nothing quite fits, at least not in any obvious way.

The central hero, all agree, is not Murphy, but rather the nearly unsung, yet nearly perfect technology-adventure-hero John Paul Stapp. Murphy himself means different things – good, bad, or enigmatic– to different people. One man, at least, is driven by the conviction that Murphy gets too much credit for Murphy's Law.

See if, with Nick Spark's help, you can make sense of it.

Marc Abrahams
Editor
Annals of Improbable Research
Cambridge, Massachusetts
January, 2006

INTRODUCTION

I have become the world's leading expert on Murphy's Law. No, really, I'm serious. You have doubtless heard the Law: Whatever can go wrong, will go wrong. To some, it is a profound statement of philosophy, a reminder that life can be defined just as much by its inherent challenges as anything else. To others the Law is a pessimistic comment underscoring, albeit in more elegant terms, the fact that shit happens.

Whatever you might think about Murphy's Law one thing is certain: it is as ubiquitous an expression as there is in American English. Over the years it has been cited in thousands of articles, websites and news reports, been the subject of several books, appeared as the title of at least one bad Charles Bronson movie and a TV show, and inspired about a zillion corollary Laws. Just about every time something goes wrong somewhere, the Law gets its two cents in.

Fortunately, my own expertise owes very little to actual adversity — I'm not writing this on life support from a hospital bed — and almost everything to research. And I don't mean laboratory research, although a bunch of people in Britain actually did try that a few years back. . .studying whether buttered toast dropped on a linty carpet has a tendency to land butter side up or, as the Law might suggest, butter side down. (Down won handily.) No, nothing like that. When I say research, I mean historical research. You see, I have become the expert on the *origins* of Murphy's Law. This happened by accident…and if I'd known what the consequences of sticking my nose into it would be - how I'd draw the wrath of famed test pilot Chuck Yeager, get caught in the middle of a nasty 40-year-old feud, and nearly wind up in a hospital bed on life support - I probably wouldn't have bothered.

Nick T. Spark
Los Angeles, California
September 2003

CHAPTER ONE *WHY THINGS GO WRONG*

Murphy's Law and Other Reasons Why Things Go Wrong
Copyright by Arthur Bloch 1977
Printed by Magnum Books

It all began a few months ago, after I showed an article I'd written for an aviation history magazine to my neighbor, David Hill. The article concerned some goings-on at Edwards, the famed Air Force flight test facility located north of Los Angeles, in the 1950's. "You know," David said, "You'd probably be real interested in talking to my father, David Hill Sr. He worked at Edwards on a bunch of rocket sled tests in the 1940's. In fact," he said proudly, "he knew Murphy."

"Murphy?" I inquired, searching my memory for a test pilot of the same name. Yeager, Crossfield, Armstrong... It didn't ring a bell.

"You know, Murphy," he went on. "The guy who invented Murphy's Law."

I didn't say it, but I was absolutely skeptical. Who wouldn't be? One might as well claim to know Kilroy or the whereabouts of Amelia Earhart. The notion seemed outright laughable. Your father knew Murphy? Sure he did! Granted, maybe someone named Murphy actually did exist at one point in time. But what are the odds that my next door neighbor's father actually knew the man? If Murphy wasn't some imaginary Irish folk hero, then he was probably a gentle sage who lived back in the 1700's. Needless to say I let the subject slide.

But a day or two later, I almost tripped over a slender book called *Murphy's Law and Other Reasons Why Things Go Wrong* that had been left on my doorstep. On the bright yellow cover, the 'r' had seemingly dropped out of "Wrong" and appeared to have smashed into the author's name, distorting it horribly. I couldn't help but chuckle at the sight of it.

The book cited Murphy's Law and then listed literally hundreds of corollaries ("Nature always sides with the hidden flaw", "Every solution breeds new problems"), commentaries ("Murphy was an optimist") and additional aphorisms such as Gumperson's Law ("The probability of anything happening is in inverse ratio to its desirability"), Cahn's Axiom ("When all else fails, read the instructions") and one that I especially admired called Gordon's Law ("If a research project is not worth doing at all, it is not worth doing well").

The extremely brief forward to the book included a letter written by an engineer named George Nichols. And this is where things got interesting. Nichols said he'd worked on a series of rocket sled tests at Edwards in the 1940's with a Colonel John Paul Stapp and that Murphy's Law emerged from these tests.

"The Law's namesake," Nichols wrote, "was Capt. Ed Murphy, a development engineer… Frustrated with a strap transducer which was malfunctioning due to an error in wiring the strain gauge bridges caused him to remark — 'if there is any way to do it wrong, he will' — referring to the technician who had wired the bridges. I assigned Murphy's Law to the statement and the associated variations…"

That appeared straightforward enough, and piqued my interest. I subsequently did some research on the internet and discovered to my surprise that the story of the origin of Murphy's Law was not something generally agreed upon. Accounts varied wildly. Some sources gave the credit solely to Ed Murphy, a man they praised for his wisdom, insight, and panache, but said almost nothing about. In other places, Nichols' letter appeared — often word for word — explaining how he had come up with "the statement." And at least a few writers suggested that Colonel Stapp, now deceased, who was at one time known as "the Fastest Man on Earth", had invented the Law.

FLIP MOVIE

To view, flip book from front to back

These frames made John P. Stapp famous. Shown in driver's education classes for generations, these images vividly portray G-forces and raw courage. Ironically, while Stapp had a tremendous impact on the life of every American, it is Murphy and his Law that are household words. Courtesy U.S. Air Force.

It made my mind race. Imagine the value, heck, imagine the importance, of learning the definitive version of the story... What were the real facts? Exactly who was Capt. Ed Murphy? What on earth was the point of the rocket sled tests? And what exactly is a strap transducer? I decided I had to find out.

How hard could it be? I thought. On the one hand, Murphy's Law might be something of an urban legend - like the story about the guy who strapped rocket bottles to his car and accidentally launched himself into a mountainside. But, on the other hand, fate and my neighbor had apparently presented me with a real link, a living, tangible person: David Hill, Sr.

CHAPTER TWO *GEE WHIZ!*

Call me superstitious, but I bring two tape recorders to my interview with David Hill Sr., just in case. When I walk into his house, I note with excitement that he has ten or so photographs of the rocket sled tests spread out on his dining room table. Yes, I think, he was really there!

The tests took place on the edge of Edwards Air Force Base, in the middle of the Mojave Desert. The photos show the test site and, beyond it, a bleak expanse of sagebrush and cacti. Beyond that, the gigantic dry Rogers Lake bed is visible. It was lakebed that made Edwards so desirable as a flight test facility. In an emergency, a pilot could land on the lakebed and save not only himself, but his plane. It was akin to having ten mile-wide runway.

The rocket sled is a primitive looking steel and aluminum car armed with four massive jet assist takeoff (JATO) rocket bottles — yes, the same type that allegedly hurtled that crazy fool into that mountain — and in the first photo Hill shows me it is shooting down a railroad track like a demon out of Hell. Behind it trails a twenty-foot long dagger of fire and a pall of grey smoke.

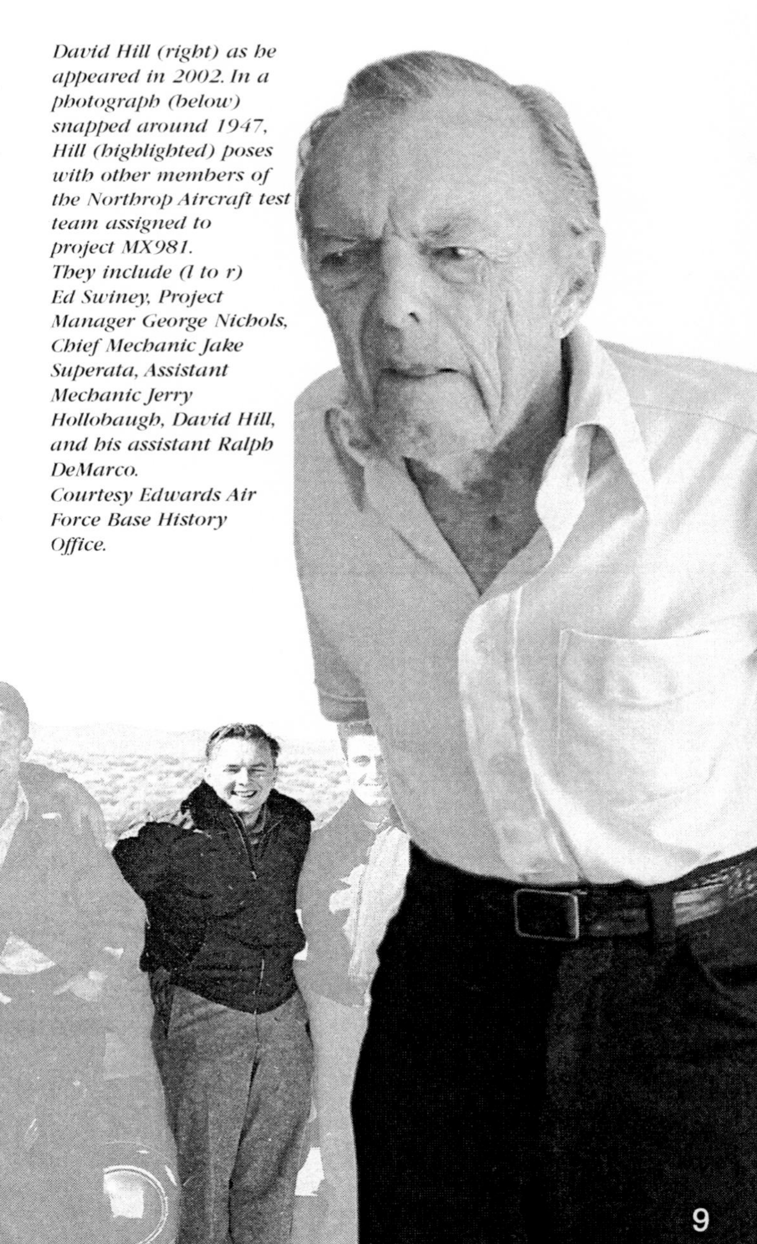

David Hill (right) as he appeared in 2002. In a photograph (below) snapped around 1947, Hill (highlighted) poses with other members of the Northrop Aircraft test team assigned to project MX981. They include (l to r) Ed Swiney, Project Manager George Nichols, Chief Mechanic Jake Superata, Assistant Mechanic Jerry Hollobaugh, David Hill, and his assistant Ralph DeMarco. Courtesy Edwards Air Force Base History Office.

"That's Captain Stapp," David Hill says, pointing to a fuzzy, helmeted figure strapped to the sled. He points him out again, this time in a group photo. Stapp is a bespeckled, smiling, somewhat pudgy man who doesn't remotely resemble the lean tough astronaut or test pilot I'd expected. "And here's George Nichols," Hill continues, pointing to a dapper, white-shirted fellow. To his right a very young David Hill Sr. squints in the bright desert sun. Is Murphy in the photo, I ask? "No," David Hill answers firmly. "I don't have any pictures of Murphy. He was only there with us a couple of days."

Although slowed by Parkinson's disease, 83-year-old Hill still has the rock solid mind of an engineer who once worked side by side with famed aircraft designer Kelly Johnson. Hill recalls events with startling clarity. Back in 1947, he'd accepted a job at Northrop and been dispatched to Muroc (later renamed Edwards AFB) to work on the top secret Project MX981. These tests were run by Captain Stapp. Stapp, Hill says with emphasis, wasn't just an Air Force officer. He was a medical doctor, a top-notch researcher, and a bit of a Renaissance man.

The goal of MX981 was to study "human deceleration". Simply put, the Air Force wanted to find out how many G's — a 'G' is the force of gravity acting on a body at sea level — a pilot could withstand in a crash and survive. For many years Hill explains, it had been believed that this limit was 18 Gs. Every military aircraft design was predicated on that statistic, yet certain incidents during WWII suggested it might be incorrect. If it was, then pilots were needlessly being put at risk.

To obtain the required data, the Aero Medical Lab at Wright Field contracted with Northrop to build a decelerator. "It was a track, just standard railroad rail set in concrete, about a half-mile long," says David Hill, pointing to one of the photos. "It had been built originally to test launch German V-1 rockets - buzz bombs - during WWII." At one end of the track engineers installed a long series of hydraulic clamps that resembled dinosaur teeth. The sled, nicknamed the "Gee Whiz", would hurtle down the track and arrive at the teeth at near maximum velocity, upwards of 200 mph. Exerting millions of pounds of force, the clamps would seize the sled and brake it to a stop in less than a second. In that heart-stopping moment, the physical forces at work would be the equivalent of those encountered in an airplane crash.

Lt. Col. John Paul Stapp circa 1953. While riding rocket sleds and improving pilot safety made him famous, Stapp's most significant contributions to American life can be felt on the highways of America: he changed how we think about automobile safety. Courtesy EAFB History Office

The brass assigned a 185-pound, absolutely fearless, incredibly tough, and altogether brainless anthropomorphic dummy named Oscar Eightball to ride the Gee Whiz. Stapp, David Hill remembers, had other ideas. On his first day on site he announced that he intended to ride the sled so that he could experience the effects of deceleration first-hand. That was a pronouncement that Hill and everyone else found shocking. "We had a lot of experts come out and look at our situation," he remembers. "And there was a person from MIT who said, if anyone gets 18Gs, they will break every bone in their body. That was kind of scary."

But the young doctor had his own theories about the tests and how they ought to be run, and his nearest direct superiors were over 1000 miles away. Stapp had done his own series of calculations, using a slide rule and his knowledge of both physics and human anatomy, and concluded that the 18 G limit was sheer nonsense. The true figure, he felt, might be twice that if not more. It might sound like heresy, but just a few months earlier someone else had proved all the experts wrong. Chuck Yeager, flying in the Bell X-1, broke the sound barrier in the same sky that sheltered the Gee Whiz track. Not only did he not turn to tapioca pudding or lose his ability to speak, as some had predicted, but he'd done it with nary a hitch. "The real barrier wasn't in the sky," he would say. "But in our knowledge and experience."

CHAPTER THREE *A FAMOUS INCIDENT REMEMBERED*

But if Stapp was a maverick, he was also a scientist and a methodical one at that. For several months Oscar Eightball rode the sled and, in the process, several major design flaws were detected and corrected. On Oscar's first trip, the primary and emergency brakes failed and the Gee Whiz shot off into the desert. On another test, Oscar was strapped in with a standard harness, and when the brakes seized the sled at 200 mph the device failed. Oscar went sailing through the air nearly 700 feet downrange and left his rubber face behind on the windscreen. Clearly, some damnable forces of physics were at work.

Finally, in December 1947, after 35 test runs with dummies and chimpanzee test subjects, Stapp got strapped into the steel chariot and took a ride himself. Only one JATO rocket bottle was used, and the brakes produced a mere 10 Gs of force. Stapp called the experience "exhilarating." Slowly, patiently, he increased the number of rockets and the stopping power of the brakes. The danger level grew with each test, but Stapp was resolute, Hill recalls, even after suffering some painful injuries. Within a few months, Stapp had not only subjected himself to 18 Gs, but to nearly *35*. That was a stunning figure, one which everyone on the test team recognized would forever change the design of airplanes and pilot restraints.

As fate would have it, David Hill was in charge of the telemetry gear that collected all of the test data. That proved to be challenging work, especially since most of the equipment was custom-made or experimental and relied on radio and electronics technologies that were still in their infancy. For one thing, most of the components contained vacuum tubes. They had a tendency to fail without warning and at the worst possible moment.

Which brings up the famous incident. At one point an Air Force engineer named Captain Murphy visited Edwards. He brought four sensors, called strain gauges, which were intended to improve the accuracy of the G-force measurements. The way Hill tells it, one of his two assistants, either Ralph DeMarco or Jerry Hollabaugh, installed the gauges on the Gee Whiz's harness.

Later Stapp made a sled run with the new sensors and they failed to work. It turned out that the strain gauges had been accidentally put in backwards, producing a zero reading. "If you take these two over here and add them together," Hill explains, "You get the correct amount of G-forces. But if you take these two and mount them together, one cancels the other out and you get zero."

It was a simple enough mistake, but Hill remembers that "Murphy was kind of miffed. And that gave rise to his observation: 'If there's any way they can do it wrong, they will.'" Despite the fact that his assistants were apparently being blamed for the mistake, Hill remembers shrugging off the comment. "I kind of chuckled and said, that's the way it goes," he sighs. "Nothing more could be done really."

Murphy soon left, but his sour comment made the rounds at the sled track. "When something goes wrong," Hill says, "The message is distributed to everyone in the program." The way the fat got chewed, Murphy's words — 'if there's any way they can do it wrong, they will' — were apparently transformed into a finer, more demonstrative "if anything can go wrong, it will." A legend had been hatched. But not yet born.

Just how did the Law get out into the world? Well, according to David Hill, John Paul Stapp held his first-ever press conference at Edwards a few weeks after the incident. As he was attempting to explain his research to a group

Stapp seen aboard the Gee Whiz rocket sled. The forward windscreen protected Stapp and acted as a stand for the high speed movie camera which, incidentally, produced the images seen in the flip book. Sitting in the rear of the sled are a set of Aerojet rocket bottles identical to those used for Jet Assisted Take Off or JATO. The circular device on the top of the sled is a telemetry antenna which, according to David Hill, worked "when it wanted to." On the bottom, below a tubular frame, one of the sled's long braking rails is visible. Courtesy EAFB History Office.

of astonished reporters, someone asked the obvious question, "How is it that no one has been severely injured – or worse – during these tests?" Stapp, who Hill remembers as being something of a showman, replied nonchalantly that "we do all of our work in consideration of Murphy's Law." When the puzzled reporters asked for a clarification Stapp defined the Law and stated, as Hill puts it, "the idea that you had to think through all possibilities before doing a test" so as to avoid disaster.

It was a defining moment. Whether Stapp realized it or not, Murphy's Law neatly summed up the point of his experiments. They were, after all, dedicated to trying to find ways to prevent bad things — aircraft accidents — from becoming worse. As in fatal. But there was a more significant meaning that touched the very core of the life mission of an engineer. From day one there had been an unacknowledged but standard experimental protocol.The test team constantly challenged each other to think up "what ifs" and to recognize the potential causes of disaster. If you could predict all the possible things that can go wrong, the thinking went, you could figure out a way to prevent catastrophe. And save John Stapp's neck.

If anything can go wrong, it will.

It was a concept that seized the cumulative imagination at the press conference. So when articles about the Gee Whiz showed up in print, Hill says, Murphy's Law was often cited right along with Newton's Second.

"I didn't think here's some profound statement that will shock the world," says Hill, expressing amazement that the remark gained such prominence. "It wasn't made as such. Of course, it's true that if there's a right way to do something, there's generally a wrong way to do it also. And it's good to recognize the difference."

To my disappointment , Hill doesn't remember much more than that. He didn't really know Murphy, he confessed. Regardless, he was sure that Murphy had passed away, as had Stapp, DeMarco, and Hollobaugh. "If anyone will know more it'll be George Nichols," he concluded. "If he's still alive, then he's the last one besides me who was there when it happened."

I tried to locate George Nichols but didn't have any luck. While continuing the search and beginning to write an article about Stapp's tests, I decided to put in a call to a friend, Edwards Air Force Base historian Ray Puffer. "You're writing an article about Stapp and Murphy's Law?" he sighs. I can literally hear his eyes rolling. As a public affairs officer, Puffer explains patiently, he's inundated with requests from all over the world to comment about it. It's a tiring, not to mention distracting, drill. "Just the other day some fellow called me from Oxford," he intones. "He's putting together a phrase dictionary and wanted me to verify the whole story. Verify it? How do you do that?"

After some gentle cajoling, Ray agrees to meet so that I can go through the archives at Edwards and see what they have about Stapp. As a bonus he offers to introduce me to Dr. Dana Kilanowski, a researcher who interviewed Stapp and is writing a book about him. "Who knows," he says drolly, "Maybe you two will get to the bottom of all this."

The highlight of my visit is a trip with Puffer and Kilanowski to see the remains of the Gee Whiz track. To get there the three of us drove out into the desolate expanse above what is called North Base. A glowing mercury-colored mirage lazes across the horizon as we bounce in Ray's car down a seldom-used dirt road. "Before we left, I called Range Safety to let them know we're out here," Ray says with a scarcely discernable smile. "They're testing some new hardware out here, and it would be a shame if we somehow got into the line of fire."

Final touches. Oscar Eightball's rubber face is lovingly installed by members of the MX981 team, just prior to another torturous ride on the Gee Whiz. Oscar and his brothers were primitive by today's standards, but proved invaluable in terms of "getting the bugs out". Later in his career, Stapp would help define specifications for dummies and supervise the first car crash tests to utilize them. Courtesy David Hill Sr. Collection.

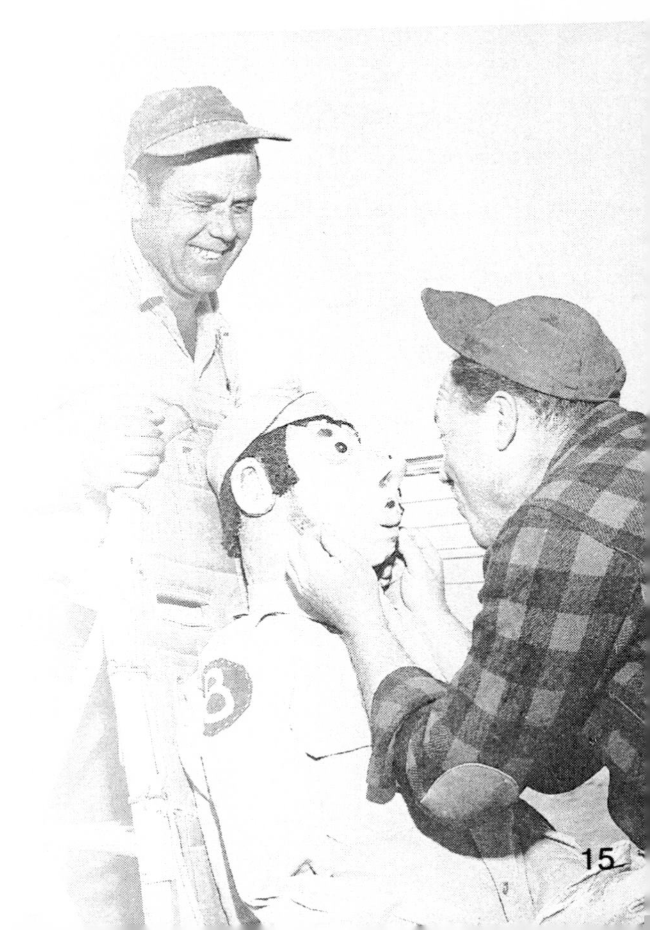

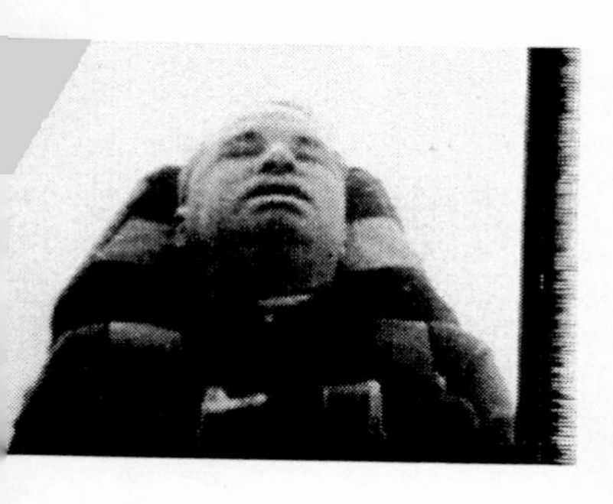

Sitting at the edge of the mighty planar lakebed near where Space Shuttles sometimes land and secret aircraft are tested, the Gee Whiz track lies forgotten amid the tumbleweeds. A surprising amount of it remains. The 2000-foot-long concrete railbed pokes out of the sand, and part of the brake stand is still extant. At the end of the track, a set of giant aircraft wheels, once part of the emergency braking system, stand forlornly amid the sagebrush. "Edwards is such a big place," Kilanowski muses, "that when they finished with a project they'd just abandon it and move to another site."

Standing at one end of the track, listening to the desert wind howl, it is hard to imagine what kind of man would willingly subject himself to the forces that Stapp endured. According to Kilanowski, the toll he took was staggering and his courage nothing short of heroic. The G-forces produced deep concussions, and the seat harness cracked his ribs and collarbone and left him bruised, battered and sometimes disoriented. "There's a famous story," she tells me later. "Stapp broke his wrist on the sled, twice. One time, being a doctor, he set the break himself on his way back to his office."

Whether Stapp showed fear or not, the tests must have been terrifying. The track was like a giant gun barrel, and Stapp was the bullet. When I speak several months later to Air Force pilot Joseph Kittinger, who worked with Stapp later in his career during Project Manhigh - where Kittinger set a world's record by parachuting from a balloon at an altitude of 102,800 feet - he calls Stapp without hesitation the "bravest man I ever met." It is a heck of a compliment coming from one of the most fearless men alive. "He knew the effects of what he was getting himself into," Kittinger says by way of explanation. "And he never hesitated."

Another rocket sled pioneer I eventually speak to, a fellow named Eli Beeding confides that, for him, the stress of the tests became so bad that he often spontaneously threw up before a run. Eventually he had to quit because of it. Yet Stapp received far worse punishment, Beeding says, and faced scarier side-effects. He never wavered. It is no wonder that around Edwards - a place known for its machismo - the soft-spoken, round-faced M.D. developed a reputation and a nickname: the "Careful Daredevil."

Some of the injuries Stapp endured, Kilanowski notes, were of a variety seldom seen and scarier as a result. At speeds above 18 G while travelling backwards (to minimize shock and whiplash Stapp faced backwards in the initial tests), he began to experience "white-outs" — a condition where blood pools in the back of the head, causing momentary loss of vision. In the forward position, Stapp suffered painful "red-outs" as the blood surged forward in his eyes and broke vulnerable capillaries. Stapp once compared the sensation to having a tooth extracted. Only it lasted for hours.

"There's only one reason he did it," Dr. Dana Kilanowski suggests. "His mission in life was to save lives. And he felt that this was one way he could do that." Both of Stapp's parents, she notes, were Baptist missionaries, and Stapp spent his childhood with them in far-off Brazil. Later in his life he'd mostly distanced himself from religion, but the missionary zeal remained.

Oscar airborne. Traveling at high velocity, Oscar Eightball shoots off the Gee Whiz — right through a wooden windscreen — and lands in a broken heap downrange. This terrible "accident" was actually intentional. Stapp used it to demonstrate the physical forces of deceleration. Courtesy David Hill Sr. Collection.

CHAPTER FIVE *SEATBELTS ANYONE?*

While saving the lives of aviators was important, Stapp realized from the outset that there were other, perhaps more important aspects to his research. His experiments proved that human beings, if properly restrained and protected, could survive an incredible impact. Yet the automobiles of the era didn't have any kind of restraints or seatbelts, even as optional equipment. Few had any safety design features to speak of. In fact, Detroit seemed not to care a whit about making safe cars. As a result most of the Big Three's autos had very solid dashboards, and steering wheels covered with ornamental badges and knobs that were utterly unforgiving in a crash. They had hardened bumpers, frames that didn't absorb any shock, and doors that tended to pop open in a collision. Without seatbelts, the occupants of a car involved in a crash were thrown around like rag dolls and often ejected. So when things went wrong, they often went very, very wrong. The carnage on American roads in the 40's, 50's and even 60's was nothing short of hideous.

Improving automobile safety was something no one in the Air Force was interested in, but Stapp gradually made it his personal crusade. Each and every time he was interviewed about the Gee Whiz, Kilanowski notes, he made sure to steer the conversation towards the less glamorous subject of automobile safety and the need for seatbelts. Gradually he began to make a difference. He invited auto makers and university researchers to view his experiments, and started a pioneering series of crash research conferences. He even managed to stage, at Air Force expense, the first-ever series of auto crash tests using dummies. When the Pentagon brass protested, Stapp sent them some statistics he'd managed to dig up. They showed that more Air Force pilots died each year in car wrecks than in plane crashes.

While Stapp didn't invent the three point auto seatbelt, he helped test and perfect it, along with a host of other auto safety appliances. Ralph Nader may have been in the spotlight when Lyndon Johnson signed the 1966 law that made seatbelts mandatory, but Stapp was in the room. It was one of his real moments of glory.

"He saved a lot of lives," says Kilanowski brightly. "In 1940 there were 25 million licensed drivers and 40,000 traffic deaths, and in 2000 there were 72 million drivers and 42,000 deaths. And I think that sums up his life. I can't imagine how many millions of lives that man's research saved over the years... He was a wonderful human being and a citizen of the world."

But what about Murphy's Law? Kilanowski says she only spoke to Stapp about the subject in passing. "They had a test run one day," she tells me, "and Captain Murphy was here from Wright Field. And the cables were set wrong, backwards. And the sled test was run and they couldn't recover any of the data. And at the time I believe Stapp said something like, 'If anything can go wrong he'll do it.' A couple days later there was a press conference in Los Angeles and Stapp said something like, 'it was Murphy's Law — if anything can go wrong, it will go wrong.'"

I'm dismayed that Dr. Kilanowski's version of the origin of the Law is so woefully incomplete. But I'm intrigued at the possibility that Stapp himself had coined the phrase. Does she really believe he did? She nods her head affirmatively. "It's very much like him," she replies. "Stapp was a man for all seasons. He had a wonderful presence about him, and was always saying wonderful things." Funny, quotable things as a matter of fact. He used to write them down and make collections of them in book form. One of Kilanowski's favorites is something known as Stapp's Ironical Paradox, AKA Stapp's Law: the universal aptitude for ineptitude makes any human accomplishment an incredible miracle. "He always thought that was too wordy and too intellectual for the general public," she laughs. "But Murphy's Law was something everyone could relate to and is more catchy."

I mention that I've read, in various and sundry accounts, that Murphy and/or Nichols is responsible for authoring the Law. "Well, I have heard that Murphy claimed he invented Murphy's Law," Kilanowski syas. "But Stapp is the one noted for his witticisms, his haiku's, and his plays on words. The base bookstore has a little book he published called *Stapp's Almanac* and there's another one called *For Your Moments of Inertia* which has pages of jokes and sayings and wit. And," she adds, "We've never heard anything else from Murphy. So I cannot imagine that Murphy developed it."

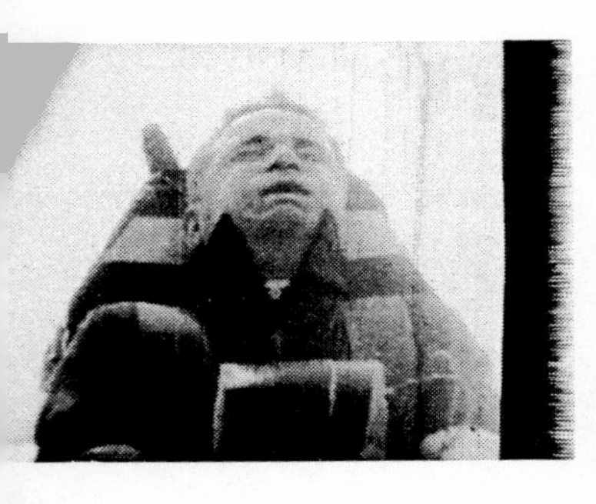

Then she throws in a kicker: "Why don't you ask George Nichols?" He is not only alive, she tells me, but living in nearby Pasadena. I can't believe my luck.

"Another person you might consider talking to is General Chuck Yeager," says Kilanowski. "He knew Stapp. They were friends."

"That's right," adds Ray Puffer, who's been quietly listening in on our conversation. "In fact, I've heard that Dr. Stapp checked on Yeager's ribs, the day before he broke the sound barrier."

To me, this bit of information is just about as big a bombshell as George Nichols being alive. Maybe bigger. Chuck Yeager is, of course, the most legendary figure at Edwards, and the biggest legend surrounding him — read *The Right Stuff* — is that he broke the sound barrier with a couple of cracked ribs. Was it really possible that Stapp examined Yeager, and okayed him for that flight? If so, it was a new and exciting revelation, and one that had never made it into the history books.

On my way out of Edwards I pick up a copy of *For Your Moments of Inertia* at the base bookstore. The title of the book, I realize, is a razo-sharp pun that reflects mightily on the career of its author. As I walk back to my car, a postcard showing Stapp on a rocket sled falls out of the binding. I look at it, and realize it is personally signed by him across the front.

I take it as a sign, and by the time I get back to Los Angeles, I'm pretty much convinced by Kilanowski's argument that Stapp is the one who refined Murphy's statement. *Moments of Inertia* doesn't cite the Law, but it is filled with wit. There are poems, limericks, and one-liners like, "Advice to Actors: Don't be a ham if you want to bring home the bacon", "Better a masochist than never been kissed", and "Lonely as a cricket with arthritis." These may sound corny as Iowa but, as a whole, the book is rather unique, impressive, and charming. If Stapp had not been distracted by his research he might have had a promising career as a writer for the *Tonight Show*.

When I call George Nichols and tell him I'd like to talk to him about John Paul Stapp and Murphy's Law, he is both excited and emotional. Stapp was one of his best friends, he explains, and he's always happy to talk about him. As for the origins of Murphy's Law, he'll talk about it but only if I agree to really pay attention. "You know, most people," he says with all seriousness, "have it all wrong."

Almost from the moment we begin speaking about John Paul Stapp, George Nichols becomes teary-eyed. Stapp's death in 1999, at the age of 89, was expected but still it hit him hard. Nichols couldn't attend the funeral because he was recovering from open heart surgery. "He was a tremendous guy," Nichols says, and a real humanitarian. He begins listing example after example. Stapp, he recounts, looked after the health of many of the dependents at Edwards who weren't entitled to Air Force medical care due to a ridiculous bit of red tape. That was typical, he says. Stapp accomplished many things off the books, against convention and military doctrine. He scrounged for equipment for the Gee Whiz crew like a corrupt supply sergeant, and defied his superiors at the Aero Medical Laboratory to advance his research. He lists example after example and concludes with this one: "When Chuck Yeager cracked his ribs before the supersonic flight, he went to see Stapp. Because he didn't believe the flight surgeons on base would permit him to fly." Stapp signed off on Yeager, Nichols continues, because he didn't believe the injury would hinder his ability to pilot the Bell X-1. "Wow," I say, pinching myself and

George Nichols, photographed in November of 2002. Photo by the Author.

making certain my two tape recorders are running. "That's an amazing story."

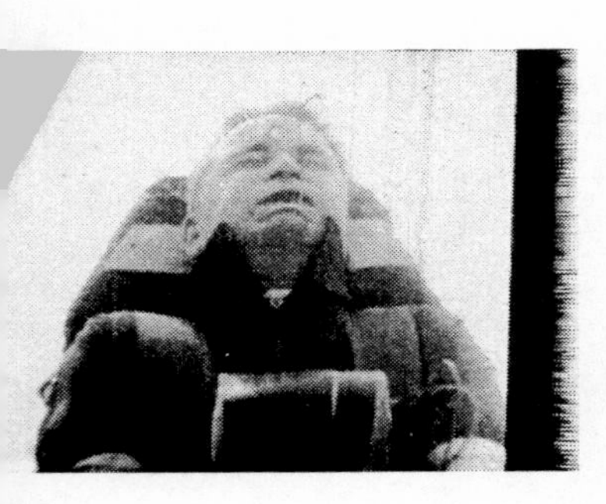

While we're on the subject of injuries, Nichols begins speaking about what Stapp endured. For all of their significance, he says, the sled tests became an awful albatross around Stapp's neck. Stapp didn't feel he would be able to live with himself if another person were injured or killed in the course of his research, so he insisted on using himself as the guinea pig for all the groundbreaking tests. As a result, he took a tremendous amount of punishment. Nichols repeats many of the incidents Kilanowski related - cracked ribs, broken wrists, concussions, bloody cysts caused by flying grains of sand - and adds one more. When the Gee Whiz tests were completed, Stapp convinced the Aero Medical Lab to build a much more sophisticated sled called the Sonic Wind at Holloman, New Mexico. On his 29th and what turned out to be final sled ride, Stapp reached a speed of 632 miles per hour — actually faster than a speeding bullet — and encountered 46.2 G's of force. In his pursuit of the knowledge of the physiological limits of the human body, Stapp hadn't just pushed the envelope, he'd mailed it to the post office.

632 miles per hour actually broke the land speed record, making Stapp the fastest man on earth. And 46.2 G's was the most any human being had ever willingly experienced. Prior to the test Nichols had real doubts about whether it was really survivable. It turned out it was, although Stapp paid a severe penalty. When the Sonic Wind stopped, he suffered a complete red out. "His eyes had hemorrhaged and were completely filled with blood," Nichols remembers, his voice cracking. "It was horrible. Absolutely horrible." Fortunately, there was little permanent damage, and a day later the visionary could see again more or less normally. He'd have a trace image in his field of vision for the rest of his life.

Bravery was one thing. But the trait that really endeared Stapp to everyone, Nichols says, was his wit. At a dismally hot, torturous, sandy place like Edwards, a little laughter went a long way. "He had an extremely unique sense of humor," says Nichols, citing his puns, limericks and especially his laws. "Now at that time there weren't a lot of laws being used," Nichols muses, "Except for the standard ones in physics and science. He started this whole business of laws. Now you've got millions of them."

Stapp's Ironical Paradox was one. Another was the 'Sunshine Law', which meant that if the sun was shining over Edwards, there must be work to do. The entire team eventually got into the act, coming up with Laws. Nichols' Law for instance came into being after he witnessed a colleague, trying to save a little time, attempt a short cut by leaping across a dry concrete canal. The attempt failed. "So my law," Nichols says proudly, "is: 'If a proposed action has any unsatisfactory results, forget about it.'" Or, as it came to be more generally known: *Avoid any action with an unacceptable outcome.*

Which leads us to Murphy's Law. The reason most people get it wrong, Nichols indicates, is that they don't know how it was originally stated or what it meant. "It's supposed to be, 'If it can happen, it will'," says Nichols, "Not 'whatever can go wrong, will go wrong.'" The difference is a subtle one, yet the meaning is clear. One is a positive statement, indicating a belief that if one can predict the bad things that might happen, steps can be taken so that they can be avoided. The other presents a much more somber, some might say fatalistic, view of reality.

A candid shot of George Nichols (dark glasses) strapping Stapp into the Gee Whiz prior to a test run. The seat on which he sits, like almost all components on the sled, was custom-built for the project. Because the Whiz would encounter tremendous G-forces on a routine basis, standard aircraft seats and other hardware were not even contemplated. Visible just above the seat frame and below Stapp's wrist is one of the connection points of his safety harness. The small rectangular shape that defines it just might be one of Edward Murphy's strain gauges. Courtesy EAFB History Office

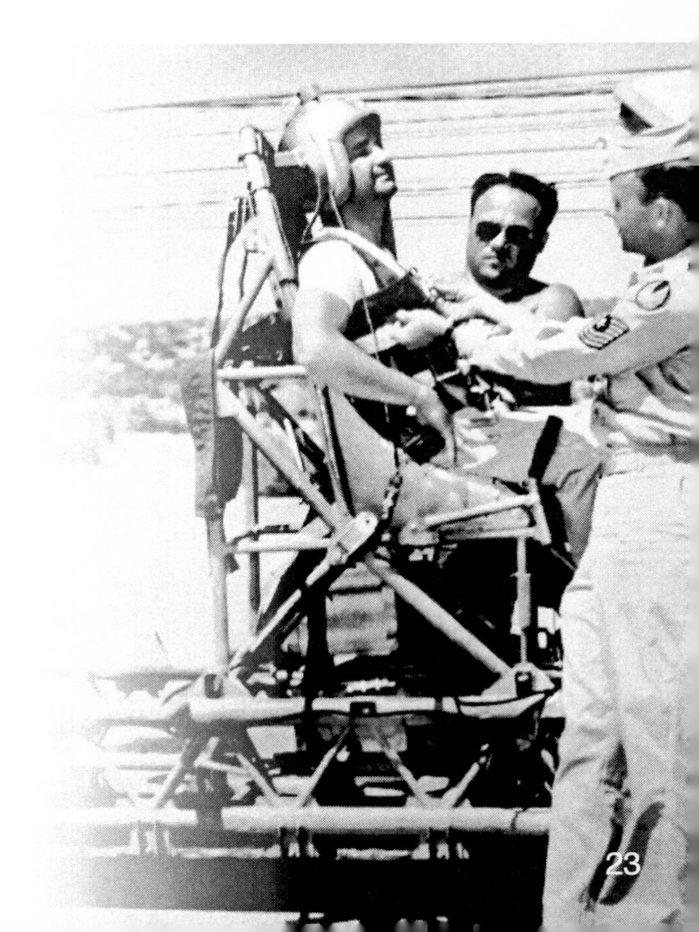

CHAPTER SEVEN *STRAIN GAUGES AND BLAME GAMES*

How did the Law come into being? Nichols relates a story similar to Hill's, only more detailed. Captain Edward A. Murphy, he says, was a West Point-trained engineer who worked at the Wright Air Development Center. "That's a totally separate facility from the Aero Med Lab," he emphasizes. "He had nothing to do with our research." Nevertheless, Murphy one day appeared at the Gee Whiz track. With him the interloper brought the strain gauge transducers that Hill described. "A transducer," Nichols says, seeing my blank look of confusion, "Is a measuring device. And these particular transducers were actually designed by Murphy."

I begin to understand the reason for Murphy's visit. His strain gauges represented a potential solution to a problem with the Gee Whiz's G-force instrumentation. Questions had been raised about the accuracy of the data obtained from sled-mounted accelerometers. What Murphy hoped to do was to actually use the test subject, be it a dummy, chimpanzee or human being, to help obtain better data. The subject always wore a restraint system consisting of a heavy harness equipped with two tightening clamps. Murphy hoped to place strain gauge bridges in two positions on each clamp. When the sled came to a stop, the bending stress placed on the clamps would be measured, and from that a highly accurate measure of G-force could be produced.

When he showed up, Murphy got Stapp's full attention. He asked if Nichols would install his transducers immediately. Not that he didn't enjoy the sunshine out at Edwards, but he wanted to return to Wright Field the next morning. "And I said, well, we really ought to calibrate them," remembers Nichols. "But Stapp said, 'No, let's take a chance. I want to see how they work.' So I said okay, we'll put them on. So, we put the straps on and took a chance on what we thought the sensitivity was."

A few hours later a test was run with a chimp, and to Nichols' surprise the chart produced by Murphy's strain gauges showed no deflection at all. "It was just a steady line like it was at zero," Nichols comments. Even if they'd been calibrated wrong, the transducers should have registered something.

"And we guessed," Nichols continues, "That there was a problem with the way the strain gauges were wired up."

An examination revealed that there were two ways the strain gauge bridges could have been assembled. If wired one way — the correct way — they would measure bending stress. In the other direction they would still function, but the bending stress reading would effectively be cancelled out. In its place would be a measure of the strap tension, which in the case of determining G force load was useless. "David Hill and Ralph DeMarco checked the wiring," Nichols continues, "and sure enough that's how they'd wired the bridges up." Backwards.

But unlike David Hill, Nichols insists that the error with the gauges had nothing to do with DeMarco, Hollabaugh, or anyone else on the Northrop team. By "they" Hill meant Capt. Murphy and his assistants at Wright Field — who had assembled the devices.

In this astonishing photo — actually a frame from a high speed motion picture camera — John Paul Stapp is caught in the teeth of a massive deceleration. One might expect a test pilot or an astronaut candidate would be riding the rocket sled. Instead there was Stapp: a mild mannered physician and diligent scientist with a wicked sense of humor.
Courtesy David Hill Sr. Collection.

The way Nichols tells it, the gauges hadn't been installed wrong - they'd actually been delivered as defective merchandise. Nichols initial thought was that Murphy had probably designed the gauges incorrectly. But there was another possibility: that he'd drawn his schematic in a way that it was unclear, causing his assistant to accidentally wire them backwards. If that's what happened, and Nichols reasoned it was likely, then the assistant had truly encountered some bad luck. He'd had a 50% chance of

wiring each gauge correctly or incorrectly, yet he'd managed to wire all four wrong. He'd defied the odds or perhaps, in some respect, he'd defined them. .. Either way, Nichols figured, Murphy was at fault because he obviously hadn't tested the gauges prior to flying out to Edwards. That ticked George off because setting up and running a test was both time-consuming, expensive, and nerve-wracking.

"When Murphy came out in the morning and we told him what happened," remembers Nichols, "He was unhappy." But much to Nichols' surprise, Murphy didn't for a moment consider his part in the error - drawing an unclear schematic. Instead, he almost spontaneously blamed the error on his nameless assistant at Wright. "If that guy has any way of making a mistake," Murphy exclaimed with disgust, "He will."

At the time, Murphy's statement didn't seem like much of anything, except a declaration of frustration and in Nichols' view, an expression of extreme hubris. Certainly no one knew a eureka moment — a "Watson, come here!" or a "The reaction is self-sustaining" — had just taken place. No one realized that the miswired transducers were like a singular destined apple, falling free of a branch and landing square on Newton's head, raising a bump and revealing a universal truth.

According to Nichols, the failure was only a momentary setback - "the strap information wasn't that important anyway," he says - and, regardless, good data from the test had been collected from the other instruments. The Northrop team rewired the gauges, calibrated them, and did another test. This time Murphy's transducers worked perfectly, producing highly reliable data. From that point forward in fact, Nichols notes, "we used them straight on" because they were such a good addition to the telemetry package. But Murphy wasn't around to witness his devices' success. He'd returned to Wright Field and never visited the Gee Whiz track ever again.

Long after he'd departed however, Murphy's comment about the mistake hung in the air like a lonely cloud over the Rogers dry lake. Part of the reason was that no one was particularly happy with Murphy, least of all Nichols. The more he thought about the incident, the more it bothered him. He became all but convinced that Murphy, and not his assistant, was at fault. Murphy had "committed several Cardinal sins" with respect to reliability engineering. He hadn't verified that the gauges had been assembled correctly prior to leaving Wright Field, he hadn't bothered to test them, and he hadn't given Nichols any time to calibrate them. "If he had done any of those things," Nichols notes dryly, "He would have avoided the fiasco."

A still frame from the high-speed movie camera mounted aboard the Gee Whiz records the agony of G-force. A typical test might involve the deceleration of the Whiz from a speed of 155 miles per hour to 34 miles per hour in a shockingly terse two-tenths of a second. Courtesy David Hill Sr. Collection.

As it was, Murphy's silly, maybe even slightly asinine comment made the rounds. "He really ticked off some team members by blaming the whole thing on his underling," Nichols says. "And we got to thinking as a group. You know? We've got a Murphy's Law in that. Then we started talking about what it should be. His statement was too long, and it really didn't fit into a Law. So we tried many different things and we finally came up with,'If it can happen, it will happen.'"

So Murphy's Law was created, more or less spontaneously, by the entire Northrop test team under the supervision of Nichols. In one sense, it represented a bit of sweet revenge exacted on Ed Murphy. But George Nichols rapidly recognized that it was far more than that. Murphy's Law was a wonderful pet phrase, an amusing quip that contained a universal truth. It proved a handy touchstone for Nichols' day-to-day work as a project manager. "If it can happen, it will happen," he says. "So you've got to go through and ask yourself, if this part fails, does this system still work, does it still do the function it is supposed to do? What are the single points of failure? Murphy's Law established the drive to put redundancy in. And that's the heart of reliability engineering."

CHAPTER EIGHT *THE MURKY PROPAGATION OF THE LAW*

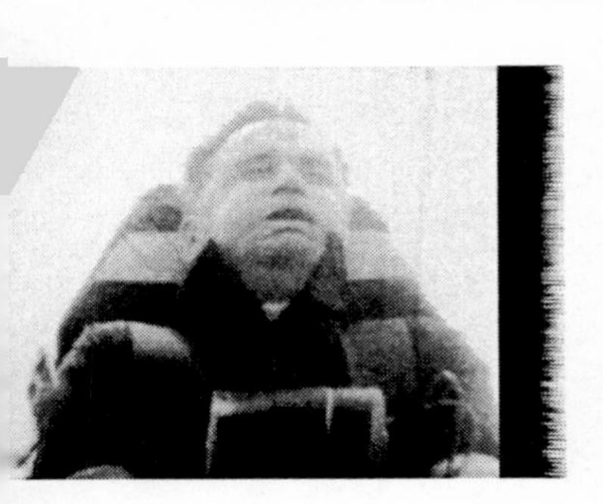

Like David Hill, Nichols says Stapp is the person who popularized the Law, via a press conference at Edwards. "Stapp said 'We're great believers in Murphy's Law'," Nichols remembers. "We spend a lot of effort making sure that the things that can cause injury in our tests don't happen." A few weeks later the phrase started showing up in articles and trade publication advertisements. "That's how it got spread out very quickly," Nichols sighs.

By the mid-1970's, when Nichols heard that a writer named Arthur Bloch was working on a "Murphy's Law" book, the phrase was ubiquitous. Yet almost no one knew its origin. So Nichols wrote a short letter of explanation, thinking that if Bloch were interested, he'd call and speak to him about it. He didn't think for a moment that the letter would become the foreword to the book and the definitive word on the subject. If he had, he might have amplified his comments.

By this time Nichols had heard a rumor that Murphy was working for Hughes Helicopter in Los Angeles, but didn't see any reason to contact him prior to the publication of the book. But when the book appeared with his letter in it, Nichols put in a call to his colleague. "And I asked him if he had seen the book," says Nichols. "And he said no, he'd heard about it. He wasn't really interested in it." Nichols was surprised, and his colleague's brusque response – annoyed was more like it – led him to question something quite basic. Up until that moment, he'd always assumed Ed Murphy knew that he was the Murphy of the Law. Now, he became convinced that Murphy hadn't a clue about it, and was completely ignorant of his legacy. "He didn't even know about Murphy's Law until Bloch published his book," Nichols says firmly. "And until I told him he was mentioned in it, he didn't even get a copy."

It's a peculiar part of an otherwise straightforward story, and of course I'm a bit surprised to hear it. It does make some sense, I reason, given that Murphy left Edwards prior to the apparent "discovery" of the Law. But that's just the beginning of a series of strange anecdotes Nichols begins to relate. Shortly after he'd contacted Murphy, he explains, things began to go seriously wrong. What should have been a nice gesture on his part produced a wholly opposite response. Murphy called and "He just went ballistic," says Nichols. "And he made this horrible, vitriolic speech in which he said that he thought Stapp and I were taking advantage of him."

According to Nichols, Murphy claimed that "what he had said that morning was a paragraph about reliability, about the use of redundancy and so on. . ."

The Gee Whiz hits the brakes hard, causing John Stapp's hair to virtually stand on end. Other details worth noting: Stapp's wearing shorts and has a high-speed camera checkerboard, used for reference purposes, painted on his shoulder and knee. Courtesy EAFB History Office.

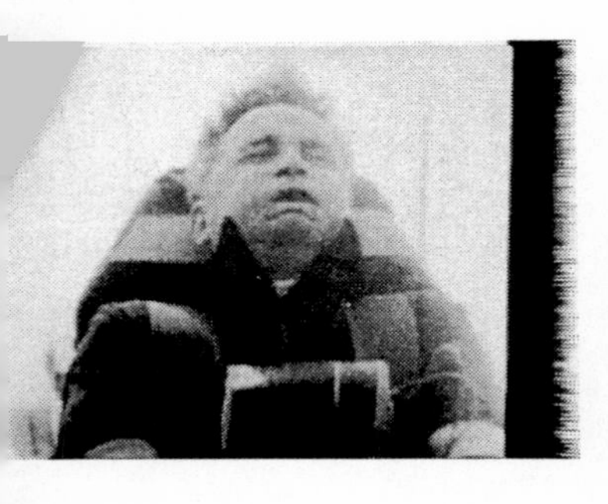

and he insisted that he had made up the Law *himself*. He also asserted that his comment that day had been intended all along as a philosophical statement about reliability. In short, he was denying Nichols' account of the discovery of Murphy's Law while attempting to stake a claim on the broad implications of it and its legacy.

A good and faithful Christian, Nichols listened to Murphy carry on, respectfully disagreed, and tried to let it go at that. But Murphy wasn't satisfied. According to Nichols, Murphy contacted a few reporters and tried to get his side of the story out in the press. He also set to work writing a short text that presented his version of events which he sent to Nichols, Stapp and for whatever reason Chuck Yeager to sign. "He wanted to put this on a plaque at West Point," Nichols recalls bitterly. "And Stapp and I talked about it, and I said this guy is trying to rewrite history. And Stapp said, 'I don't like that and I'm not going to support it.'"

At that point, Nichols felt Murphy had crossed a line, but he was still willing to forgive him. But then Murphy's wife called Nichols and made some desultory statements about him and Stapp. She accused both of them of making money off of the Law, something Nichols says was "absurd". Then she roundly chastised them for not agreeing to sign the plaque. Stapp had suffered so many concussions in his lifetime, she implied, that he obviously couldn't remember what had transpired. A short time later, Murphy called again and according to Nichols "he tore me apart. Then he tore Stapp apart. And he tried to take credit for (the Law)." That was the last straw. Nichols hung up the phone and never spoke to either Murphy or his wife again. Murphy died in 1989, Nichols says, his voice quavering a bit. "And that was the end of that... It was very, very intense," he says sadly. "And it just ruined it. I used to look back on some of this as a good memory."

I'm relieved when Nichols reaches the end of the story. By now he's gotten himself pretty worked up, and in the back of my mind I've been remembering that he'd told me he'd only recently had heart bypass surgery. I can just picture it now, the paramedics and their defibrillators, and me trying to explain that this is all a result of Murphy's Law.

Members of the Gee Whiz rocket sled team pose at Muroc (Edwards AFB) North Base in 1948.
Sgt. Harry Goniprouskis (front row)is one of the few people who volunteered to ride the sled in support of the tests.
Courtesy EAFB History Office.

David Hill Jerry Hollabaugh George Nichols unknown person Jake Superata Ralph DeMarco

Ed Swiney Schmidt (first name unknown) unknown person Sgt. Harry Goniprouskis

Capt. John Paul Stapp.

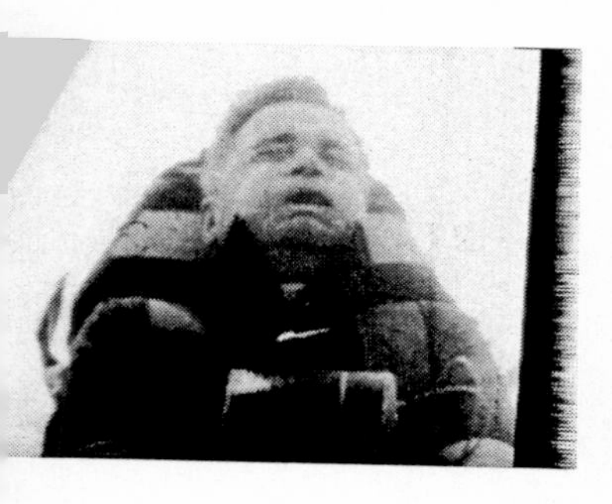

To record detailed information on impact velocities over different parts of his body, Stapp wore accelerometers on his knee, chest, and in his mouth. Courtesy EAFB History Office.

Fortunately, Nichols rapidly collects himself, and starts talking about more positive things, such as how he once used Murphy's Law as an example in a Bible study class. He grows cheerful as he returns to the subject of his friendship with John Stapp, and notes how the man's patience, integrity, and humility inspired him throughout his own career. "He didn't seek any publicity for what we were doing," he elucidates, "Except when he felt it was important for people." Stapp was featured in an article in *Time* magazine, Nichols notes, and his work inspired a Hollywood B-movie called *Towards the Unknown*. "He only agreed to these things because he thought it might help persuade people that seatbelts were necessary," Nichols says. "It wasn't for his ego." In fact at one point Stapp's friends played what they thought would be a nice trick on him by arranging an appearance on the television show *This is Your Life*. He shocked everyone by walking off the set.

Then the engineer grows somber again. "Of course he paid a price for what he did," Nichols laments. "Not just a physical one." Despite his best efforts, Nichols explains, Stapp became a celebrity of sorts. The Air Force brass didn't like the attention he was getting, and when he used his fame to chastise auto manufacturers, he made enemies in Detroit and in Congress. Eventually, there was a reckoning, and Stapp was re-assigned by the Air Force to a position where he was effectively marginalized. In short, Nichols implies, Stapp's brilliant career and his quest to save human lives was cut short by jealousy and politics.

It's time I take my leave. Driving home, I can't help but think how my opinion of John Paul Stapp has grown mightily while talking to Nichols. Yet at the same time, my vision of Murphy has been completely shattered. The person Nichols described was not a charming, silver-tongued Irish rogue with a unique sense of humor and amazing insight, as I had wanted to believe. He was apparently a pompous, jealous toad, someone who might actually have been so dour as to believe that "whatever can go wrong, will go wrong."

At the same time, I'm not altogether surprised to hear that Murphy might have gone off the deep end in the immediate aftermath of Bloch's book being published. To have a bestselling novelty book, not to mention that bad action movie and all those calendars and t-shirts, sold with your name on them — and not to get a dime out of it! — that would be really irritating.

Anyway, after talking with Nichols, I feel I know a lot more about the Law. But I'm also keenly aware I've only heard one side of the story. What if Murphy really had come up with the Law, as some people claimed? And what if I trusted what Nichols said but, in reality, he was the one modifying the truth? And all because Murphy simply wasn't around to defend himself. An old saying keeps coming to mind: History is told by the winners. Now I find myself coining an appropriate corollary, a Spark's Law if you will: History is told by the survivors.

I put in a call to West Point to see if they might be able to help me find any of Murphy's descendents. I don't make much progress, but I do wind up with a copy of a page from the 1939 West Point yearbook. In it is a photograph of a dashing Edward Aloysius Murphy in full dress and, below that, a picture of him tinkering with a large, gas-powered model airplane. "Our earliest memory of Murph," the *Howitzer* notes in a short tribute, "is of a plebe convulsed with laughter at the antics of the Beast Detail." That, certainly, seemed closer to how one might imagine *the Murphy* – a man with a sense of humor. And in that context, the next line of the tribute seemed eerily prescient: "Abounding with ideas, (Murphy) sought new solutions for each problem, and he enjoyed nothing so much as an argument on his methods. Murf's originality amused and amazed us; his friendly grin won a place in our memory." It was a fascinating description, especially the part about his ingenuity and need to debate his methods. But what stayed with me was that last comment about his grin. Just like the Chesire Cat's persistent smile …

EDWARD ALOYSIUS MURPHY

BENICIA, CALIFORNIA

Senatorial

Our earliest memory of Murf is of a plebe convulsed with laughter at the antics of the Beast Detail. Clutching his sense of humor, he scurried through the Academy never more than one jump ahead in academics, but never too harried to entertain with his polished imitations. Abounding with ideas, he sought new solutions for each problem, and he enjoyed nothing so much as an argument on his methods. Murf's originality amused and amazed us, his friendly grin won a place in our memory. "Murf"

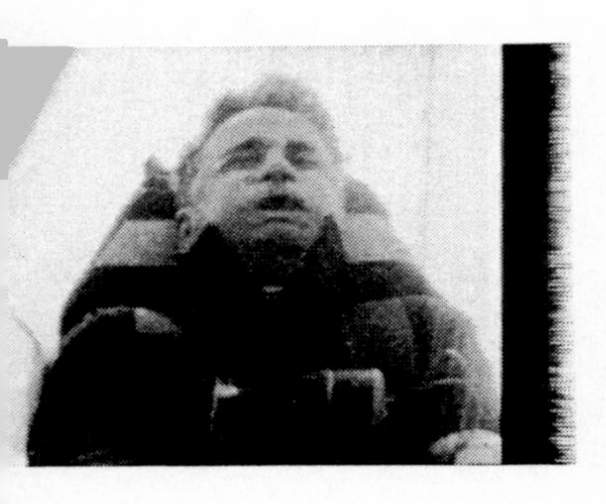

A week later, I do some old fashioned research in the library. I find a number of magazine and newspaper articles written about John Paul Stapp, including the issue of *Time* Nichols mentioned. It features a cartoonish cover depicting "Space Surgeon Stapp" as a giant disembodied head riding on a rocket sled. The article discusses John Stapp's career and mentions a number of his eccentricities, such as the fact that he could play the bassoon, spoke several languages, and had been so poor that, as a college student, he once ate a guinea pig carcass left over from a dissection lab. That's decidedly weird, but what surprises me more is that neither this article, nor any of the others I find dating back to 1948, mentions anything about Murphy's Law. When exactly did the press conference that Hill and Nichols so vividly remember actually take place?

I make one truly tantalizing discovery. In the *Los Angeles Times* there is a letter to the editor written a few weeks after John Stapp's death by a Mr. Robert Murphy. It references Stapp's obit and says, "Thank you for including a reference to 'Murphy's Law' and correctly attributing it to my father, Edward A. Murphy (1918-1989)." The letter went on to say that the obit's description of the origin of the Law — which pretty much matched Nichols' — was incorrect. "It was not Murphy who 'rigged a harness incorrectly,'" wrote Robert Murphy. "It was a technician on his test team who will forever go nameless. The sensor harness mistake was the classic of being absolutely wrong. Sensors intended to switch 'on' the instant the rocket sled test started were incorrectly connected to switch 'off.'"

On and off, I wonder? Where did he come up with that? I'm at a bit of a loss, and it actually crosses my mind that this Robert Murphy might be some kind of impostor. Of course, I have to find him first. I figure, heck it should be easy. There's probably only a few million Bob Murphys in the world... I just have to write letters of inquiry to them all.

But fate, coupled with some serious elbow grease, works in mysterious ways. I get in touch with Robert Murphy, and he quickly convinces me he really is the son of Ed — he just knows too many details to be lying. He tells me to track down a particular issue of *People* magazine featuring his father, and a book by Lawrence Peter — the man behind the Peter Principle ("In a hierarchy every employee tends to rise to his level of incompetence") — called *Why Things Go Wrong*. These two texts, he says, present definitive versions of events from his father's perspective. When I've looked at those, he promises me, we'll meet and chat.

Dragon's teeth. Shown here are the matching sets of brake shoes, capable of exerting thousands of pounds of force upon the sled's braking rails. In case of a hydraulic failure, a restraining cable similar to those used for aircraft arresting gear would be deployed. Courtesy EAFB History Office.

I track down both texts. In the *People* article (dedicated to the "unsung sage of the screw-up") Murphy more or less described what Nichols had, although some details varied. He said there were six, not four, strain gauges used on the sled, and that Stapp, and not a chimp, had been riding the sled at the time of the malfunction. He also emphasized that the failure of the gauges was a hugely expensive error, something Nichols had taken pains to deny.

Most significantly, Murphy said that after the error was revealed he'd declared, "If there's more than one way to do a job, and one of those ways will result in disaster, then somebody will do it that way." At that moment, Murphy claimed, a much-inspired John Stapp proclaimed (eureka!): "That . . . is Murphy's Law."

I fully expected the Lawrence Peter book to repeat this account, but it doesn't. Instead, it gives credit for the Law to "George Nichols . . . who happened to be present when Murphy uttered these words . . . and dubbed the remark Murphy's Law."

CHAPTER TEN *CATCHING UP WITH A REAL MURPHY*

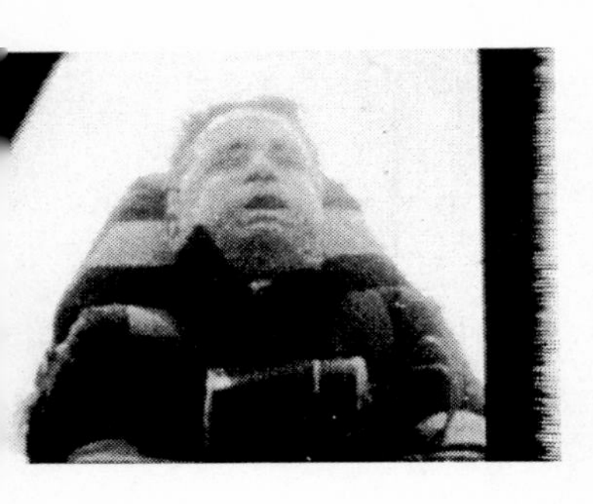

Robert Murphy is a little less enthusiastic about talking to me than I am about talking to him, mainly because the subject of Murphy's Law — well, it turns out it gets old after a few decades. It's not a blessing or a curse, Murphy explains, but inquiries from curious parties like myself are not altogether infrequent. Yet, at the same time, even his closest friends don't believe him when he explains that he isn't just the son of "a Murphy", but of *the* Murphy. It's a strange and, in some ways, obvious predicament. If Ed Murphy had a less common Irish surname, like Clancarty, maybe people would be inclined to believe him more. But then again, would something called Clancarty's Law have spread like wildfire? Probably not.

Edward A. Murphy Jr. was born in the Panama Canal Zone, Robert tells me. From the beginning, he had been groomed to be an Army man like his father, a goal he fulfilled when he was accepted into West Point. By then the clouds of conflict were gathering and shortly after he graduated, Murphy was swept up into the chaos of World War II. He knew how to fly planes, but his real talent lay in engineering. As a result, he became a chief maintenance officer. He ended up stationed at various bomber bases on the China, Burma, and India theatre - known as the CBI. He flew over "the Hump", and fixed planes from Saigon to Mandalay.

At war's end Murphy was dispatched to Wright Field where, Robert tells me, he worked closely with John Stapp. He was an integral part of Stapp's test team. "My father would make frequent trips to Muroc," he says. "And come back and analyze the results." Later, his father was transferred to Norton, and then to Holloman AFB. If he'd stayed in the Air Force at that point, Murphy speculates, his father probably would have supported Stapp's work on the Sonic Wind. "We lived right next door to Dr. Stapp at Holloman," he recalls. "In fact my sister and I used to raise mice and other animals for use in his lab." But the Murphy family's time in New Mexico was short lived. Murphy left the Air Force in 1954 for a better job in the civilian world, becoming a human factors engineer for Douglas Aircraft. He then worked for a series of companies before retiring from Hughes Helicopter, where he was a reliability engineer. "That was part of the application that he'd done all along,"

Robert concludes. "But it's kind of ironic that Murphy's Law would come from a reliability engineer."

I ask Robert Murphy to share the story of the origins of the Law, as far as he knows it. What emerges is a slipshod version, and one I sense he isn't quite comfortable telling. There aren't "on" and "off" switches this time, but the details are sketchy. One interesting part of the story revolves around the idea that all the wires in the infamous transducer were identical, such that it was possible to connect them incorrectly. If some of them had been red, or some fatter than others, he says, then it would have been impossible to wire them backwards. "So the design was bad." When I ask him to expand on this a bit more, he politely declines, and refers me to the account in Lawrence Peter's book. In a sense I'm relieved when he does. The last thing I want to hear is another, completely different version of these hallowed events.

"Anyway," Robert Murphy says broadly, "It is a reliability statement. If it can be done wrong, then somebody is going to do it wrong. That's one interpretation of Murphy's Law that's pretty close to what he meant. If you can design something and one way to assemble it or screw it in or whatever is going to make it fail," Robert sighs, "Then the design is wrong."

Robert says he's somewhat offended at the implication that his father mistreated George Nichols, and is surprised to hear that they had a falling out. It's nothing he's ever heard anything about. "I don't think my father ever claimed he'd actually come up with the Law," he says. "I mean, it's named after him." On the other hand, he suggests, Nichols might have his own reasons for raising a fuss — to try to lay claim to the Law's legacy.

An early view of the Gee Whiz sled, seen here equipped with a fully-enclosed passenger compartment. This was later removed to facilitate high speed photography and presumably because it was really, really hot inside. Courtesy EAFB History Office.

Robert's never heard of the incident with the West Point plaque, and dismisses it as a non-event. "The whole idea of my father campaigning for a plaque is completely against character," he says matter-of-factly. "He never pushed the fact that he was "the Murphy". In fact, I didn't realize it for years." Despite that comment and all that it might imply, Robert doesn't buy the idea that his father was wholly ignorant of the Law either, as Nichols claimed. "We lived next door to John Stapp at Holloman," he points out. "And I'm sure if he didn't know about it by then, Stapp must have mentioned it to him."

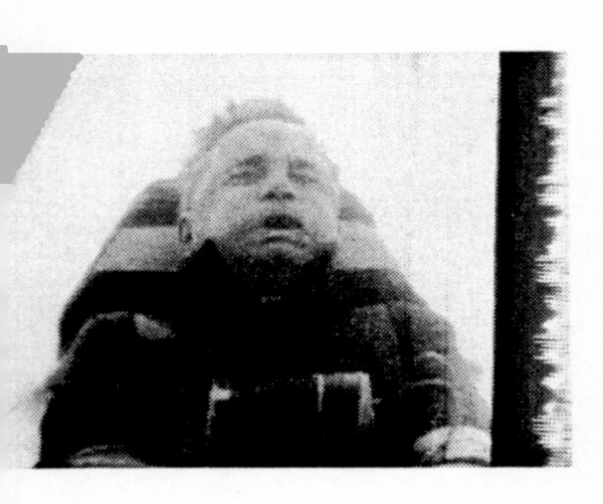

I move on to other topics, since Robert clearly doesn't know anything about the feud. Robert relates how, as a Murphy, he tends to notice references to the Law with frequency. "I see some version of it at least twice a month," he suggests. "There's one in this morning's paper, in fact, the headline about the Harrier airplanes that have been crashing? It happens all the time. But interestingly enough," he says, in between sips of coffee, "I worked in Japan for two and a half years and they had no idea about Murphy's Law. They had never heard of it, and they didn't get it." That turned out to be an amusing cultural anomaly, not to mention a striking irony. After all, the reason Robert Murphy went to Japan in the first place — he worked there as a technical writer — was to prevent typos from showing up in the literature made by an auto manufacturer. This same manufacturer had an embarrassing incident occur just a few years prior: all the owners' manuals for their cars contained the words "five speed shitting transmission" instead of shifting.

John Paul Stapp manages a grin, and George Nichols closes the door to the Gee Whiz's passenger compartment. The four large JATOs visible underneath the sled indicate this was a major test ride. Courtesy EAFB History Office and author's collection.

Robert relates a few other tantalizing tidbits about Ed Murphy. In 1954, he

came home with a heavy duty harness designed for a jet fighter and installed it in the family's Studebaker. At that time, it was probably the only car in the country to have a seatbelt. Another thing Robert remembers is that his father covered his golf balls with fluorescent paint. The paint, which had only recently been developed to facilitate high speed photography of rocket sleds, allowed him to play golf in the twilight. "People used to laugh at him because he had these silly colored golf balls," Robert says. "Now they're everywhere." So if his father had missed the money train by not copyrighting Murphy's Law, he might have redeemed himself by patenting the Day-Glo golf ball. But, alas, the thought probably never crossed his mind.

Robert tells me one last anectdote before we part. "You know my father became good friends with Lawrence Peter? Right. Well, Peter was going to contact Parkinson. You know, Parkinson's Law?" Robert says. "'Work expands to meet the time and money that is available.'" Having the three of them together would have been a heck of an historical moment, I have to admit. Unfortunately, the meeting never took place because naturally, something came up.

CHAPTER ELEVEN *BREAKING THE TRUTH BARRIER*

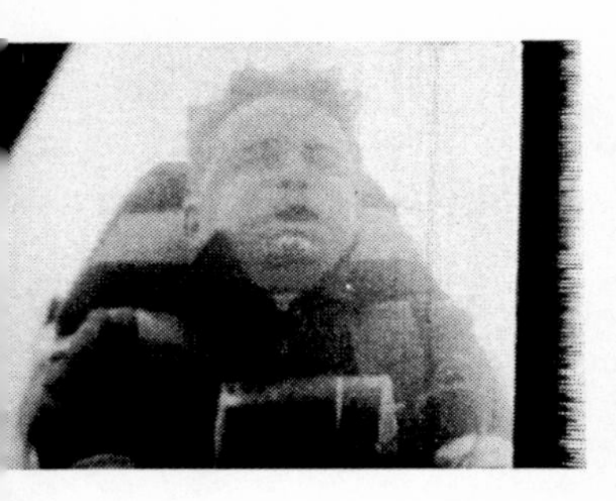

A few interesting events transpire in weeks following my meeting with Robert Murphy. The first is that I get ahold of General Chuck Yeager. I'd sent him a letter way back when, never expecting he'll actually contact me. When he does and I have him on the phone, I feel my blood pressure rise. I can't believe I'm talking to the one, the only, true legend of Edwards.

Yeager has fond memories of Stapp and considered him a friend. At one point he even took Stapp up in a jet plane and opened up the rear canopy so that Stapp could experience first hand the effects of wind blast that a pilot would encounter in an ejection. Yeager remembers inviting the good doctor over to his home for dinner on at least one occasion. The real motivation, he confesses, wasn't good conversation. It was so that Stapp could give cursory medical examinations to his young sons who weren't permitted to receive medical care at Edwards.

The conversation is flowing along, but when I ask Yeager whether Stapp ever checked his ribs, prior to the supersonic flight, the General's attitude instantly changes. "Who told you that?" he says forcefully. "That's a bunch of crap!"

I explain I have it from two different sources, although I'm not entirely certain they're credible. There is a brief pause on the phone, and then Yeager responds gruffly, "That's the way rumors get started, by these people...who weren't even there. Guys become, if you'll pardon my expression, sexual intellectuals. You know what the phrase is for that?" I admit to Yeager that, no, I'm not exactly familiar with the phrase. Sexual what? "Sexual intellectuals," he says. "They're f—ing know-it-alls, that's what."

I'm almost afraid to ask my next question, which is whether Yeager is familiar with Murphy's Law, and knows that it came out of Stapp's work. "Well," Yeager says in a clipped voice. "I'm familiar with it. But I don't associate that with Dr. Stapp." There is another brief silence, and then he cautions me, "Look, what you're getting into here is like a Pandora's Box. Goddamn it, that's the same kind of crap…you get out of guys who were not involved and came in many years after. It's just like Tom Brokaw's book if you'll pardon the analogy here, about the best of the breed or something like that. Every guy who wrote his story about World War II did it fifty years after it happened."

"I'm a victim of the same damn thing," Yeager goes on, a bit less vitriolic. "I tell it the way I remember it, but that's not the way it happened. I go back and I read a report that I wrote 55 years ago and I say, hmm, I'd better tell that story a little bit different. Well, that's human nature," he continues reflectively. "You tell it the way you believe it and that's not necessarily the way it happened. There's nothing more true than that." He laughs and our conversation is at an end.

Despite how badly my interview with the legend went, I feel strangely relieved. I don't feel let down that I've failed to find a definitive answer con-

The business end of the Sonic Wind. A much more sophisticated sled than the Gee Whiz, it was designed to carry up to twelve massive rocket bottles and could travel into the supersonic range. Stapp told everyone it was a "wonderful test instrument", but there was no question what it really was: a lean, mean machine designed to race towards the edge of the envelope and the unknown. Courtesy EAFB History Office.

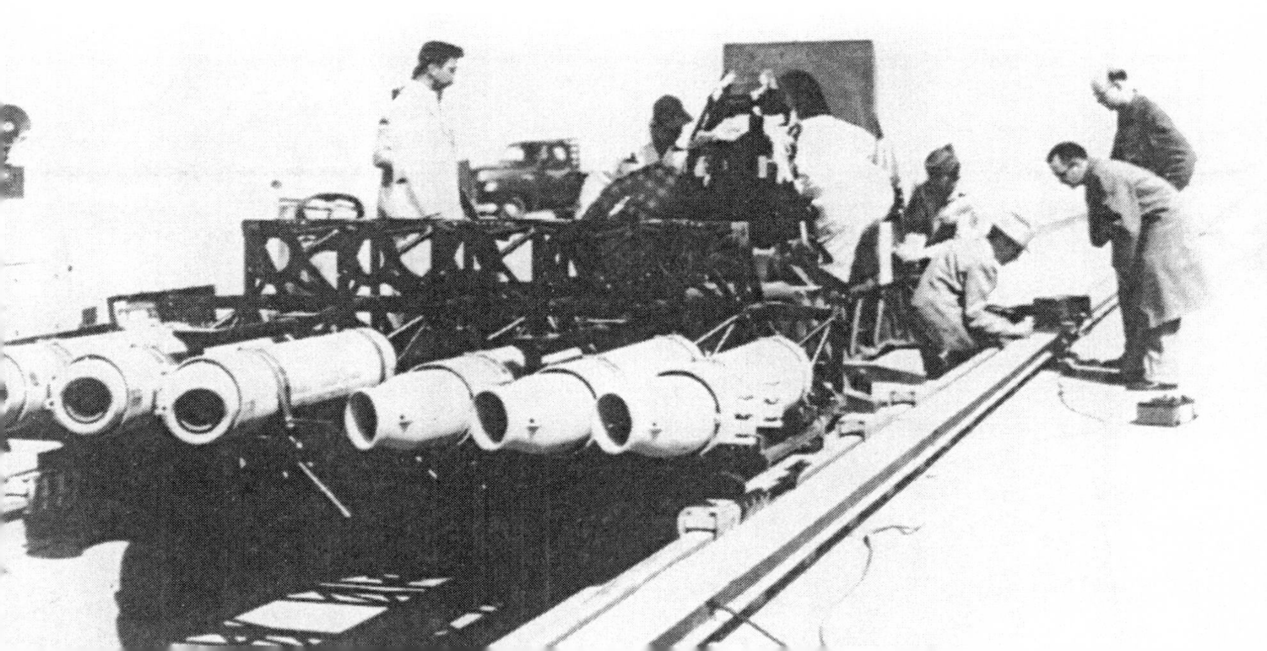

cerning the origins of the Law because Yeager's right: there is no definitive truth. History, as the old saying goes, is nothing more than a pack of lies that everyone agrees are true.

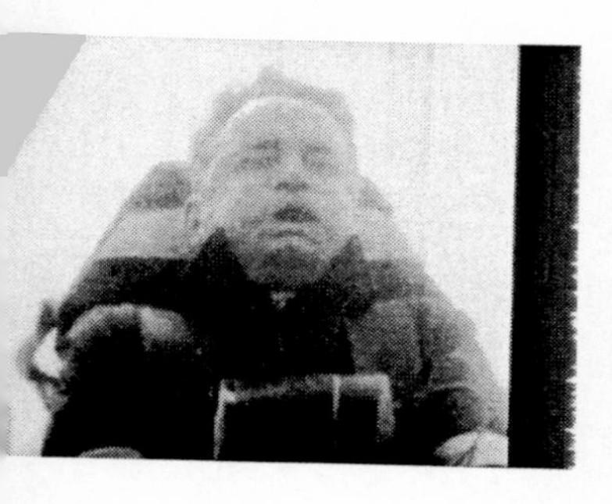

In the case of insignificant or personal history especially, the truth is usually too boring to make it through the rewrites, and to thin to keep from falling through the cracks or dissipating from sheer forces of entropy. Imagine a game of whispering down the lane that lasts fifty years: by the time a generation has passed, it's hard to separate fact and fiction, insignificant event from defining moment, and villain from hero. Not to mention average Joe, from hero. The truth is, I think, that even if John Paul Stapp and Ed Murphy were still alive, I probably wouldn't be able to learn the real story behind the Law.

CHAPTER TWELVE *THE VOICE OF MURPHY*

Then I received a series of intriguing emails from Robert Murphy. In one he wrote that he wanted to clarify that his father passed away in 1990, not 1989 as he'd written in his letter to the *Los Angeles Times*. In another he wrote that he'd found a note from the President of the Los Angeles West Point Society stationery asking "if they could possibly make a plaque about Murphy's Law for possible submission to the Academy. In other words," the email continued, "(the plaque) was not something my father was campaigning for. As I told you, self-promotion was completely foreign to him." In the same email Robert cited the comments I made at our meeting about George Nichols and said that in his view, "George Nichols is just an angry old man who regrets that the Law was not named after him, nothing more. He is a self-tainted source."

And then Robert wrote an email containing some exciting news. He'd been going through some things — I'd asked him to please find a photo of his father — and he'd come across a cassette tape of a radio interview his father had given about the Law. I quickly arrange a meeting. Over a cup of coffee and a slice of pie, Robert presents the tape along with an 8x10 glossy photo of his father working on an ejection seat prototype.

The cassette tape is unmarked, and there is no spoken introduction whatsoever on the recording. I guess it might be the CBC, or NPR, and probably dates from the time of the *People* article, the early 1980's. It's as close as I'm going to get to interviewing Ed Murphy, and of course I can't wait to hear it.

"Yes, Virginia," says the nameless commentator broadly, "there really is a Murphy. Ed Murphy, who we've got on the phone today. . ."

Ed Murphy's voice is serious, deliberate and humorless. Absolutely appro-

John Paul Stapp aboard the Sonic Wind on December 10, 1954, just prior to breaking the land speed record and enduring 46.2 G's of force. Pilot Joe Kittinger, who would fly a chase plane during the test, told a reporter that if Stapp survived, "It'd be as significant a human accomplishment as breaking the four minute mile." Courtesy EAFB History Office.

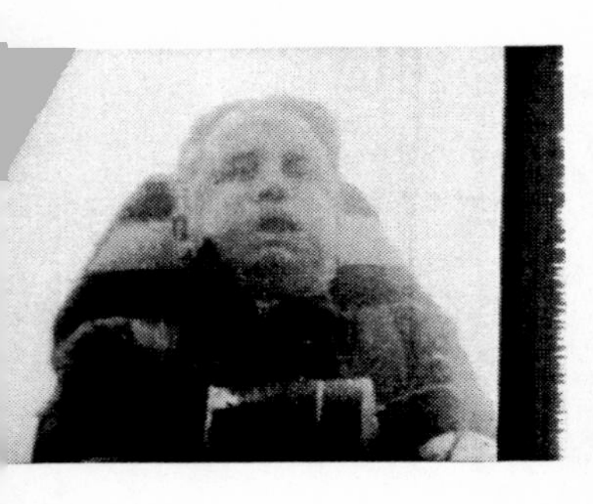

priate, I decide, for a career engineer. Asked to tell his version of the Murphy's Law story, he goes into the kind of excruciating detail you'd expect from someone obsessed with precision. It leaves the interviewer, who apparently believed he was going to speak with a slick, witty personality, completely flummoxed.

Right off the bat Murphy explains in the interview that, as Nichols and Hill stated, he wasn't part of the Gee Whiz team. He'd only been to Edwards once during Stapp's tests. He'd been working at Wright Field on a project similar to Stapp's but which involved the use of a large centrifuge instead of a rocket sled. He'd designed some innovative electronic measuring equipment for the centrifuge and, when John Stapp heard about that, he asked if Murphy'd design similar components for the Gee Whiz. Murphy leapt at the chance because he admired Stapp and the groundbreaking work he was doing.

The way Murphy tells it, he sent his equipment out to Edwards and it worked well for a few tests. But then something went wrong. Stapp called him to say that he'd "risked his neck riding on that darn sled" and the instruments had produced no data. "So I got on the next airplane to Muroc and had a meeting with him," Murphy explains. "And I said all right, let's see the accelerometers." An examination of the accelerometers revealed to Murphy that — like Hill said — "they had put the strain gauges on the transducers ninety degrees off."

Yet contrary to what Nichols said about Murphy not taking the blame for the trouble, Murphy admits in the interview that he felt - to a certain degree - it was his fault. "I had made very accurate drawings of the thing for them, and discussed it with the people who were going to put them together, but I hadn't covered everything," he sighs. "I didn't tell them that they had positively to orient them in only one direction. So I guess about that time I said, 'Well, I really have made a terrible mistake here, I didn't cover every possibility.' And about that time, Major Stapp says, well, that's a good candidate for Murphy's Law. I thought he was going to court martial me," Murphy notes dryly. "But that's all he said."

When a confused Murphy wound up the courage to ask Stapp what he meant by 'Murphy's Law', Stapp reeled off a host of other Laws, and said smartly that "from now on we're going to have things done according to Murphy's Law."

"And that," Ed Murphy wraps up, "is about the way I think it happened."

Murphy's explanation is five minutes long and full of confusing technical information. Interestingly, while reciting these facts, Ed Murphy didn't bother to state his own Law. So when the interviewer finally gets a word in edgewise, he doesn't know what to say except that "There is now a new Murphy's Law and this is it: you ask Captain Edward Aloysius Murphy a question and by God you get an answer!"

As Stapp waits resolutely, final preparations are made by the crew at Holloman Air Force Base for what would turn out to be the researcher's greatest - and final - rocket sled run. Courtesy EAFB History Office.

Then the interviewer tries to pin Ed down. "Now most people," he says, "think that Murphy's Law goes like this: if anything can go wrong, it will. Is that right?"

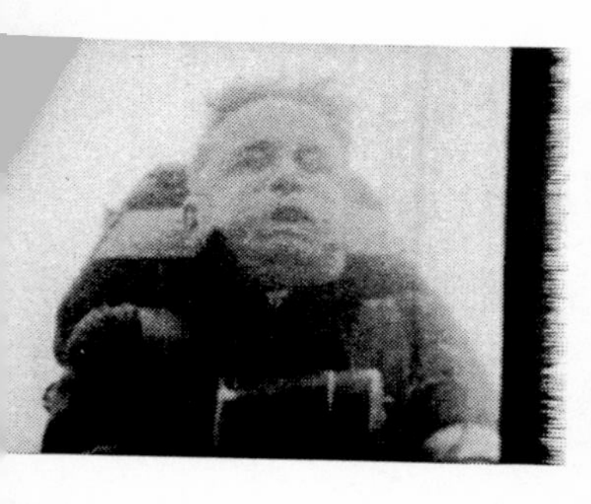

"Well," Murphy replies, "I wouldn't say it's wrong."

"But how did you say it originally?" the interviewer teases.

"About that way. But I wouldn't say that's exactly the words," Murphy retorts. "I don't remember. It happened thirty-five years ago, you know."

"Okay," the interviewer concedes. "Tell me the truth. Are you tired of being asked about it?"

"No," says Ed Murphy, just before signing off. "I enjoy it. I make a lot of friends that way. Everybody likes to think, that they have discovered a wonderful thing ... when they hear Murphy's Law for the first time."

The Sonic Wind hits the water brake. When the sled came to a rest and it turned out Stapp was still alive, George Nichols, the Northrop team and many in the Air Force breathed a sigh of relief. Stapp longed to do another test — this time at Mach 1.0 — but cooler heads prevailed. It was fortunate they did. Just a short time later, while performing another test without a human passenger, the Sonic Wind left the track and was nearly destroyed. Courtesy EAFB History Office.

MURPHY'S LAW APPLIED TO MURPHY'S LAW CHAPTER THIRTEEN

It's true, I think: Murphy's Law is a wonderful thing and something which, many centuries down the line, will probably still be quoted with regularity. It is a universal truth, a highly reliable precept, applicable to almost any situation. My own included. Where the story of the origin of the Law is concerned I conclude, I couldn't possibly have hoped to get it right. At least that's the lesson I'm forced to draw. If Murphy's Law can be seen as a statement about entropy, human frailty or fallibility, then the contradictory story of its origins is annoying but also altogether apropos.

Indeed, when I think back on the "facts" I've managed to gather, all I can do is smirk. Few stand up to scrutiny. Nichols might have written in Bloch's book that he coined the term "Murphy's Law". Yet during our interview he described it as more of a group effort. Murphy claimed in *People* and in his radio interview that Stapp named the Law, but apparently told Lawrence Peter that Nichols had done it. And while Nichols had claimed that Murphy had tried to usurp the Law, I couldn't find any direct evidence of that. Just as I couldn't find any evidence that Stapp had ever mentioned Murphy's Law at a press conference, despite what both David Hill and Nichols told me.

In similar fashion, Hill told me the words Murphy uttered after the failure were "If there's any way they can do it wrong, they will." Whereas Nichols claimed it was "If there's any way he can do it wrong, he will". Yet when Murphy told the story to Peters, he claimed he'd said, "If there's more than one way to do a job, and one of those ways will end in disaster, then somebody will do it that way..." He'd told the radio interviewer something entirely different – "I really have made a terrible mistake here, I didn't cover every possibility" – and when pressed, he said he couldn't remember just what he'd said.

I could go on. While Ed Murphy blamed himself for the mistake, Hill blamed DeMarco and/or Hollobaugh, and Nichols blamed Murphy's assistant at Wright Field and/or Murphy – although for different reasons than Murphy did! While Nichols said there were four strain gauges, that their failure wasn't a big deal, and that a chimp was involved, Murphy said there were six gauges, and that the failure was an extremely costly mistake which occurred while Stapp rode the sled. Similarly, Murphy said he wasn't there when the transducers initially failed, but Nichols and Hill said he was. Robert Murphy apparently once believed the failure that inspired the Law involved "On" and "Off" switches, Kilanowski believed Stapp had coined the phrase, and Ray Puffer thought Stapp'd examined Yeager's ribs... Well, I think you get the point. It all depends whose story you want to believe.

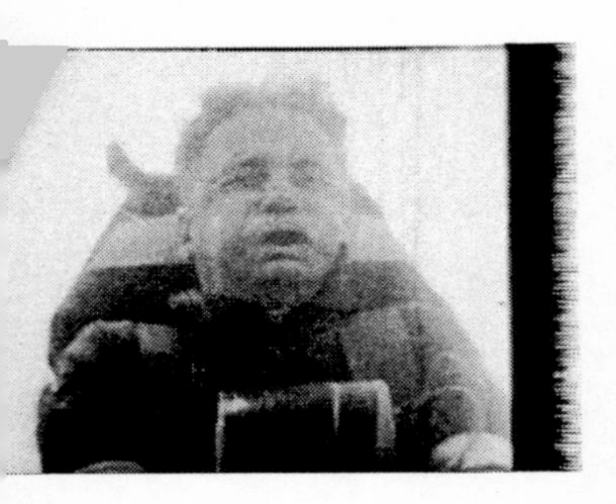

There are at least – some – undeniable facts. No matter who was at fault or who named the expression, The Law was named in honor of Ed Murphy, that's for sure. And Stapp was almost certainly the person who popularized it. Without Stapp's showmanship at that fateful press conference (true I couldn't find any evidence of it, but it must have happened), without his Promethean effort at contextualizing the Law and showing the world it was a universal truth, it probably would have vanished into the ether.

It's a notion I think about when something truly scary happens to me. I'm driving down a four lane road at the speed limit, and I idly change lanes. Everything looks all clear, but suddenly my car is hit from behind with terrific force and goes spinning all the way across the street into the curb. Later, reconstructing events, I realize that the other driver, who was speed-

In this North American Aviation factory photo, Edward A. Murphy and an unidentified cohort prepare an ejection seat, possibly a model developed for the F-107, in 1957. While Murphy labored in relative obscurity, the Law that bears his name became well-known throughout the world during his lifetime. And while his contribution to the Gee Whiz tests was fairly minor, his name will forever be intertwined with those of Hill, Stapp, and Nichols, and his amazingly versatile Law will probably still be quoted centuries from now.

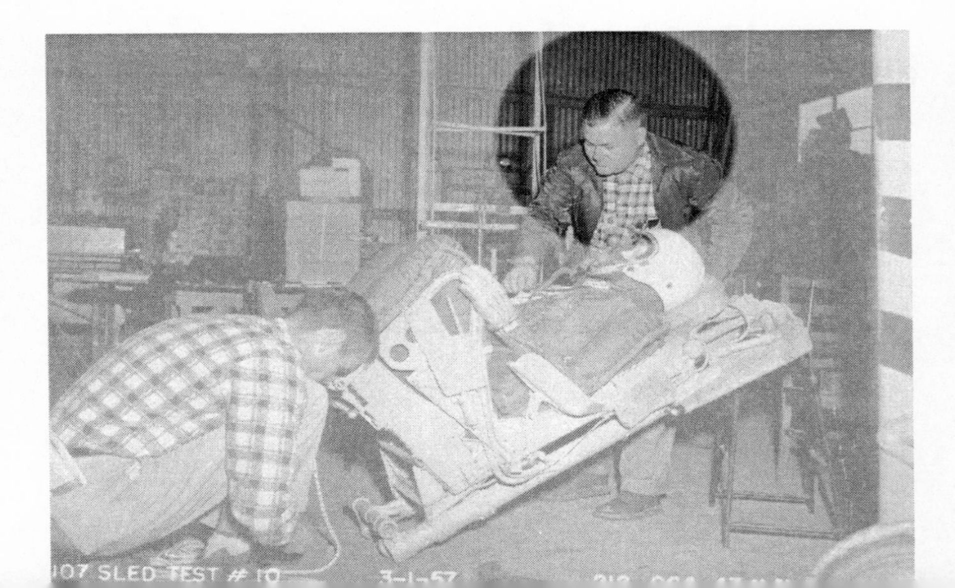

ing at a good twenty miles above the limit, changed lanes to pass me at the exact same time I changed lanes. There was seemingly no way I could have seen him, and he was traveling too fast to stop or avoid hitting my car. I can't shake the thought: whatever can go wrong . . .

My car is nearly totaled — the rear crumple zone is completely compressed — but because of that and my shoulder harness seatbelt I walk away uninjured. It's a miracle really. And as I sit on the curb and wait for the police to arrive, I can't help but think about John Paul Stapp's steadfast, tireless efforts in the cause of auto safety. He might not have invented Murphy's Law, achieved "household word" fame or semantic immortality, but Stapp's contributions are real and remain with us in the present day.

In that sense, Stapp is the true hero of the Law. He's a ghost in the machine of every modern airplane and automobile, making sure that when things go wrong - really wrong - they don't become much worse. So, sitting there on the curb, I say a silent thank you to the man who risked his own life in an effort to save thousands of others. My own included. John Paul Stapp was a courageous man, a great man I think, and his legacy continues to grow with each passing day.

Today Edward A. Murphy Jr. rests quietly in a veteran's cemetery. But his legacy continues to grow with each passing day. Whether or not he coined the Law, whether it was named in his honor or out of spite, Ed Murphy's amazingly adaptable Law continues to persist, and its appeal shows no signs of abating. Photo by the Author.

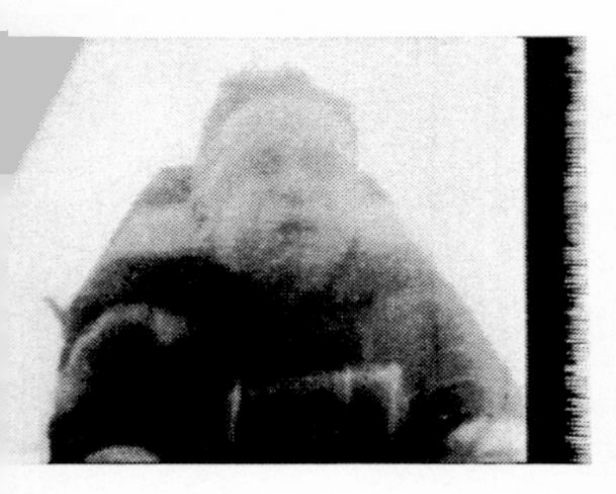

It was never actually my intention to chronicle the history of Murphy's Law. When several years ago David Hill told me that his father David Sr. worked at Edwards AFB on rocket sled tests with John Paul Stapp and a guy named Murphy, it was the words "Edwards" and "rocket sled" that got my attention. I often write for aviation history magazines, and this sounded like perfect fodder for my editors. Murphy's Law did not. But, as I researched Stapp's career, the subject of the Law invariably came up. Slowly, I began to think of the story not as an urban legend, but as something that might have actually happened. It roused my sense of curiosity, and long after I had written in detail about rocket sleds and g-forces, I continued to probe the story surrounding the origins of the aphorism.

Of course I knew where to submit articles about rocket sleds. But an article about Murphy's Law, well it proved nearly impossible to place. Just as I was about to abandon hope Marc Abrahams, the editor of the Cambridge, Massachusetts-based *Annals of Improbable Research*, called. He informed me that he not only wanted to publish the piece, but actually hoped to rush it to press. It would appear in the very next issue of the *A.I.R.* "I'm not allowed," Marc said cryptically, "to tell you exactly why I want to print it right away – it has to remain a secret for now. Just let me say something related to your article, something important, is in the works."

I was delighted that the *A.I.R.* would publish the article, even if Marc proposed to pay the princely sum of $0 for the right to do it. The *Annals* is a magazine full of wit, vinegar, lively debates about the chicken and the egg, and altogether dubious science. In short, it's the kind of publication that John Paul Stapp might have been proud to affiliate with. Some of his *For Your Moments of Inertia* wisdom - bits of insight like "If chimpanzees could talk, we would soon wish that they wouldn't," or worse "A bridge builder should be judged by his piers" - could have easily graced its pages.

Soon a package containing a dozen copies of the "Murphy's Law Special Issue" arrived at my apartment. Imagine my surprise to discover that every one was missing staples in the spine, and the center pages to boot. A phone call revealed that this was not a practical joke but a genuine printing error. "Believe me," Marc intoned seriously, "This has never happened before. It must be the Law at work."

That wasn't the kind of remark I needed to hear. While many friends expressed amusement at my "research", others warned that nothing good could come of toying with something as karmically disruptive as the Law. So I was relieved when, after the piece appeared in print and on the Internet, very little seemed to go wrong. Most comments were congratulatory and friendly. Of course, there were a few cheeky e-mailers and one or two whose sanity seemed suspect. There were also several hundred obligatory notes from people who wanted to share examples of Murphy's Law in action, discuss the rocket car legend, or who noticed typos and felt obligated to point them out with a clever postscript such as "don't worry we all make mistakes" or "Murphy's Law strikes again!"

Not all the emails were so glib. Many thoughtful people wrote concerning the Law's philosophical implications. "Isn't Murphy's Law just further proof," commented one, "that humans tend to remember the bad, especially the really bad, over the good?" Another added, "I think it's quite telling and says something about the human condition that it wasn't written, 'Whatever can go right, just might.'" Still another expressed delight with one particular point made by the article: "The fact that Murphy's Law can actually be something of an optimistic statement - a way to gain awareness and focus our lives in order to prevent things from going wrong - never occurred to me. I'm going to keep that in mind from now on."

Scientists and engineers appeared to have a sincere interest in the article and the Law. "The important thing to remember about engineering," one wrote, "is that things just go one way or another, not wrong or right. The engineer's task is to guide the result toward something useful for the design purpose at hand." Mathematician Robert Matthews, who conducted experiments proving it is more likely that dropped buttered toast tends to land butter side down more often than not (owing apparently to wind resistance factors), also wrote an insightful note that I'd like to cite here. Unfortunately, I deleted it by mistake.

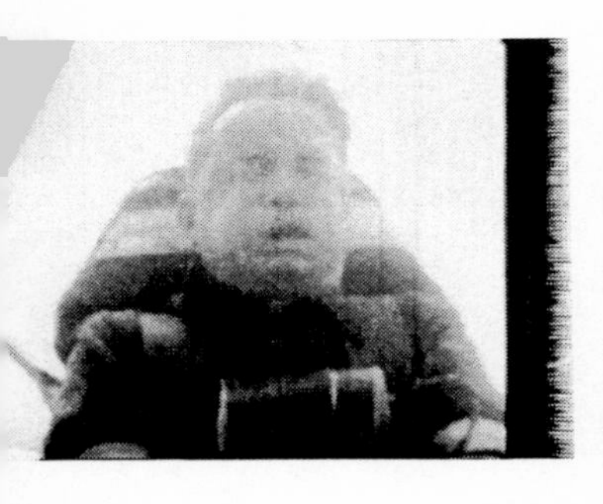

Other correspondents supplied favorite variations on the Law, wrote about it as a universal truth, demonstrated its applicability in almost any profession or situation, or offered astute observations. "In 50,000 years," one self-appointed prophet commented, "people, or more likely the robots that replace the error-prone people, will still be cracking each other up with it. Anytime something goes wrong they'll blame Murphy the programmer."

Another e-mailer wrote to me about Edward Murphy's mysterious doppelganger, Edsel. Yes, according to certain Internet sites, it was "Edsel Murphy" who discovered the Law. The notion that Murphy's Law could be affiliated with the Ford Motor Company's biggest design debacle seems funny and almost predictable. As do the rumors forwarded to me by a handful of concerned readers, stating that they'd heard Murphy had died an altogether horrible, accidental death in a car crash / airplane crash / ice skating accident. Out of respect for the Murphy family's privacy, I never did ask exactly how Edward A. left this world, but I'm pretty sure it was peaceful.

QUESTIONS AND REACTIONS

To my surprise, only a handful of correspondents directly questioned whether Murphy's Law really originated at Edwards. Predictably, most supplied a counter story. A fellow named Burgess for example wrote that his father worked as a radio operator during WWII and that "something called Finagle's Law – 'anything that can go wrong will' – was common knowledge among radio operators. One night in honor of a bartender on an island in the Caribbean the name was changed to Murphy." There is not much one can say about this sort of story. A series of Finagle's Laws do exist, and are apparently about as old as Murphy's, but I doubt they have anything to do with bartenders. Still, I should point out Finagle's Second Law is a personal favorite and seems apropos in this instance: "No matter what the anticipated result, there will always be someone eager to misinterpret it, fake it, or believe it happened according to his own pet theory."

Another correspondent from the United Kingdom indicated he felt the phrase "Murphy's Law" had a prejudicial overtone, leading him to suspect it originated much earlier than the 1940's. "In the Nineteenth and Twentieth Centuries," he elucidated, "the Irish were frequently the butt of ethnic jokes on both sides of the Atlantic. The drunkard Murphy, O'Rourke or O'Doul is a typical protagonist. Frankly," he continued, "I see every reason to question your research, as I tend not to believe that Murphy's Law has a modern origin. You did not discuss this at all in your article, but it seems likely to me that Murphy's Law originated centuries ago."

Another person voicing doubts was Fred Shapiro, the editor of the *Yale Dictionary of Quotations*. This soon-to-be-published tome will explore famous sayings from the dawn of recorded history. Fred wrote that in his opinion the origins of the Law may have predated World War II and that "if the Nichols / Murphy / Stapp story of the origin of 'Murphy's Law' is correct, it would be part of the 1% of undocumented colorful etymological stories that are factual." From his perspective, my research should have relied less on interviews with people like Hill and Nichols, and more on library studies. "The real riddle of Murphy's Law," Shapiro summarized, "is that if the Nichols account is correct, why is there no documented evidence [in print] of 'Murphy's Law' before 1955? Beyond that, why was there no mention of the Nichols-Stapp-Murphy story until 1976 when Arthur

Edward A. Murphy III is seen while giving the keynote address at the Ig Nobel Awards at Harvard University. Other recipients of Ig Nobels that night were Lal Bihari of Pradesh, India, who received the Peace Prize for leading an active life even though he had been legally declared dead, and Yukio Hirose who received the Chemistry Prize for analyzing the composition of a statue that pigeons would not land upon. Courtesy of the Annals of Improbable Research.

Bloch's Murphy's Law book was published? How many true stories are first noted 27 years after the fact?"

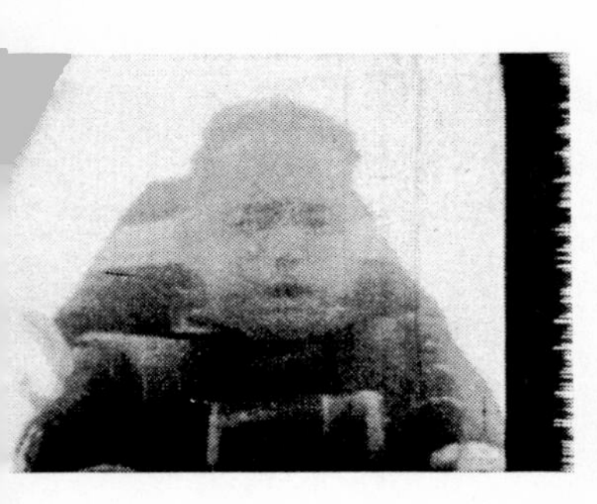

I had to admit I had not invested much time trying to determine when the Law first appeared in print, and I asked Mr. Shapiro if he had anything to say about the subject. Quite a bit, it turned out. The first known reference specifically to Murphy's Law, he informed me, appeared in the May 1955 issue of the *Aviation Mechanics Bulletin*. It was defined this way: "If an aircraft part can be installed incorrectly, someone will install it that way." Three months prior to that the more common precept, "Anything that can go wrong, will go wrong" appeared in print for the first time. The venue was a short story in *Astounding Science Fiction* called "Design Flaw", where the phrase was termed "Reilly's Law."

I found Shapiro's scholarship interesting, but did not immediately pursue his leads. I had my hands full with a number of other projects. One of them was trying to get George Nichols to calm down. He didn't like the article one bit and appeared genuinely upset that I had not promoted his version of events as definitive. "You're giving a voice to Murphy and empowering him," George told me, a hint of anger in his voice. "He didn't ever tell the goddamned truth." I tried to explain that I perceived my role to be that of a journalist, not as a jurist. That while I personally believed his version of events was probably accurate, it was beyond my power to fully authenticate it. He didn't want to hear that. "You're promoting his lies," George chastised. "That's all there is to it."

Robert Murphy's reaction was painfully similar: he felt I'd done him and his father an awful disservice by including Nichols' version of events. "You could have written an article that told the truth and clarified things for all time," he railed at me on the phone. "Instead you chose to promote something entirely different." Robert was especially dismissive of the reasons I gave as to why the article contained Nichols' account. "That explanation makes no sense. Look, it's common sense: it's called Murphy's Law, not Nichols' law," he said. "It's named after my father."

I replied that I'd never disputed that the Law was either named by, or in honor of, his father, and that the article made that quite clear. Yet at the same time I pointed out that his father's accounts appeared inconsistent, and were directly contradicted by Nichols. "Well, you shouldn't believe anything he says," Robert concluded sourly. "He's just a disgruntled old man who wants what he can't have, and that's to have his name connected with this for all time."

In retrospect, the level of anger and bitterness expressed by Nichols and Murphy should not have surprised me. It was nevertheless disappointing. Eventually however, I began to view the dissolution of their friendship with me as proof that I must have succeeded in telling a fairly balanced version of events.

About this time, incidentally, I was put in touch with John Stapp's widow Lilly. I sent her a copy of the article hoping she might make some comments. It turned out that she didn't have much to add because she hadn't even known Stapp at the time it was coined. She did remember that her husband was irritated by the attention it seemed to get and the trouble it caused, and said so many times. "He didn't understand," she confided, "why there was so much fuss about it. You know, don't people have more important things to do with their lives?"

On the plus side, my neighbor David Hill reported that his father David Sr.

Edward A. Murphy III accepts the Ig Nobel Engineering Prize from Nobel Laureate William Lipscomb. Author Nick T. Spark appears on the left. Courtesy of the Annals of Improbable Research.

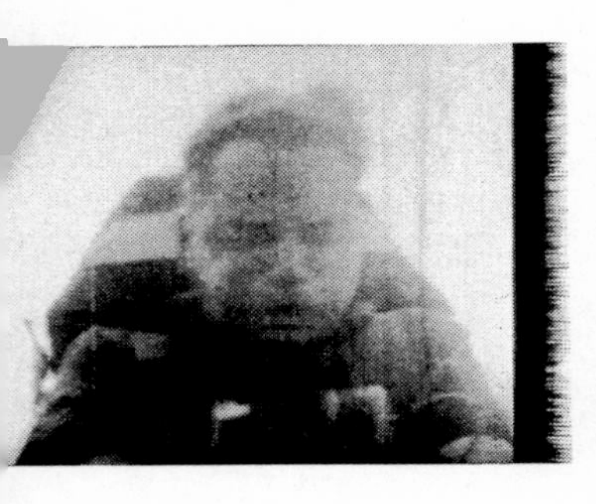

thought the piece was terrific. "We showed your articles to him and he loved them," he told me. "Especially he enjoyed reading about Murphy." The issue of *A.I.R.* put David Hill Sr. in such a good mood that David Jr. brought up a favorite, but forbidden, topic: Groom Lake or, as it is more commonly known, Area 51 - the top secret government facility located in the Nevada desert. Somehow David Jr. knew that his father once worked there, and whenever his father's guard was down, he'd ask about it. Usually the request was greeted with stony silence. But this time David Hill Sr. leaned forward and said, "Groom Lake. All right already. You want to know about Groom Lake, I'll tell you something about Groom Lake." He waved his son to come close, and then whispered in his ear. "They make," he said, "a damn good piece of banana cream pie at Groom Lake."

MURPHY RECEIVES A DUBIOUS HONOR

While David Hill Sr. never did clarify the mystery surrounding Area 51, Marc Abrahams finally did explain why he'd been so excited about publishing my article. It turned out that a few months before I'd sent it in, Ed Murphy and his Law had been selected by a secret committee of the A.I.R. for a rather prestigious honor: the Ig Nobel Prize. Not to be confused with the Nobel, the Ig is something the society inflicts, er, awards every year for achievements in science that as the press release puts it, "first make people LAUGH, and then make them THINK."

Now, thanks to background information contained in my article, the *A.I.R.* would award the honor not just to Murphy, but to John Paul Stapp and George Nichols for "jointly giving birth to" the maxim. Representatives of all three would be invited to Harvard for the presentation. As things turned out this would include Ed Murphy's eldest son Edward, whom I'd never met. Lilly Stapp was kind enough to appoint me as ambassador for her late husband. It would be an honor to represent one of my personal heroes in Cambridge.

George Nichols could not make the trip, but wasn't disappointed about missing the Igs. I spoke to him on the phone, and he told me that he believed the entire event was designed to promote Murphy's side of the story. "They're going to let a Murphy give the keynote address," he told me. "That should tell you everything you need to know." Eventually Marc persuaded George that the occasion could represent an opportunity to tell his side of the story, and he relented somewhat, agreeing to send a pre-recorded acceptance speech to Harvard for the ceremony.

Just prior to the Ig Nobel presentation, I met Edward Murphy III. Like his brother Robert he had very little patience for my article. He indicated that he owned papers, saved from his father's estate that might shed considerable light on the origins of the Law. However, he refused to share them with me, suggesting that I was already tainted by Nichols and that, in his eyes, I was merely an "opportunist" who hoped to benefit from affiliating myself with his father's discovery.

In spite of this tumult, the Igs turned out to be a wonderful event. The presenters included actual Nobel Prize winners, and the audience consisted of hundreds of rowdy, paper-airplane-throwing Harvard students. Fellow recipients of the Ig included some Aussie Ph.D.'s who wrote a physics paper entitled, "An Analysis of the Force Required to Drag Sheep Over Various Surfaces", a charming Dutch researcher named C.W. Moeliker who documented "The First Case of Homosexual Necrophilia in the Mallard Duck" and Karl Schwarzler who accepted the Economics prize for developing a means by which the entire tiny nation of Lichtenstein could be rented out for corporate events or an altogether unforgettable bar mitzvah.

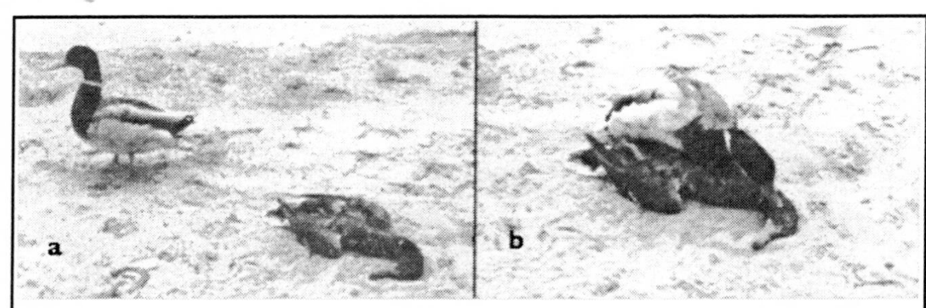

Figure 2 **a** Drake mallard (*Anas platyrhynchos*) in full breeding plumage (left) next to the dead drake mallard (NMR 9997-00232) just after collision with the new wing of the Natuurmuseum Rotterdam. **b** the same couple during copulation, two minutes after photo **a** was taken. [photo: C.W. Moeliker]

The 2003 Ig Nobel Prize for Biology went to C.W. Moeliker, a Dutch researcher who documented the first-known case of homosexual necrophilia involving mallard ducks. Courtesy C.W. Moeliker.

Edward Murphy III's keynote speech, which George Nichols dreaded, turned out to be both brief and wholly appropriate. Edward focused on the fact that his father always defined the Law as a positive, and not a fatalistic statement. Failure may or may not be inevitable, he noted, but it does present opportunities. Furthermore, it is important to understand the significance of failure in any scientific or worldly endeavor. Such things, he noted, are "not pre-ordained but preventable."

Moments later, Ed Murphy accompanied me to the podium and, under a near-constant rain of paper airplanes, made a few brief remarks before gratefully accepting the Ig. No one was there to accept the award on behalf of George Nichols, but nevertheless his gravelly voice boomed through the auditorium via cassette tape. He reiterated that the Law came into being as a consequence of two "critical mistakes" made by Edward A. Murphy.

When it was my turn I said, "I'm here accepting tonight for Col. John Paul Stapp, on behalf of his wife Lilly. Col Stapp risked his life to make seatbelts in automobiles a reality. He may or may not have been responsible for naming Murphy's Law. From his perspective, the Law serves as a warning: think about what can go wrong, and what you can do in advance to prevent that from happening."

Then I accepted the Ig Nobel: a clear plastic box containing a solid, 22 karat gold bar measuring exactly one nanometer square.

AFTERMATH: TO THE Nth DEGREE

For a long time after the Ig Nobel ceremony, I continued to respond to emails and requests for information and photographs related to Dr. Stapp, his research, and Ed Murphy. While answering one of these inquiries, it occurred to me that I should locate the issue of *Astounding Science Fiction* that Fred Shapiro mentioned contained an early version of the Law. As soon as I got it, I flipped to the index, found the story "Design Flaw" by author Lee Correy, and read with interest.

Just as Shapiro indicated, on page 54 a "Reilly's Law" is mentioned. It surfaces in a discussion between fictional aerospace engineer Guy Barclay and KX-238 project manager Don Karlter, who notably enough are discussing a subject dear to George Nichols' and Ed Murphy's hearts: reliability.

(Karlter) drummed the desk top with his fingernails. "Boys, here at White Sands our toughest problem has always been reliability. It's difficult to get something to work the same way every time. Some engineering sciences have licked the reliability problem but it looks like we're stuck with it."

"Reilly's Law," Guy said cryptically.

"Huh?"

"Reilly's Law," Guy repeated, "It states that any scientific or engineering endeavor, anything that can go wrong will go wrong."

"Very true in rocketry," Karlter admitted. "So we've got to put in components we know to be reliable to the nth degree."

Certainly Reilly's Law and the commonly stated variant of Murphy's Law appeared identical. But while Fred Shapiro perceived the citation in *Astounding Science Fiction* as evidence that neither Murphy, Stapp nor Nichols coined the Law, it did little to shake my own convictions.

More recently, while preparing to write this afterword in fact, I had the notion to type the name of the author of "Design Flaw" – Lee Correy – into

Excerpt from "Design Flaw"

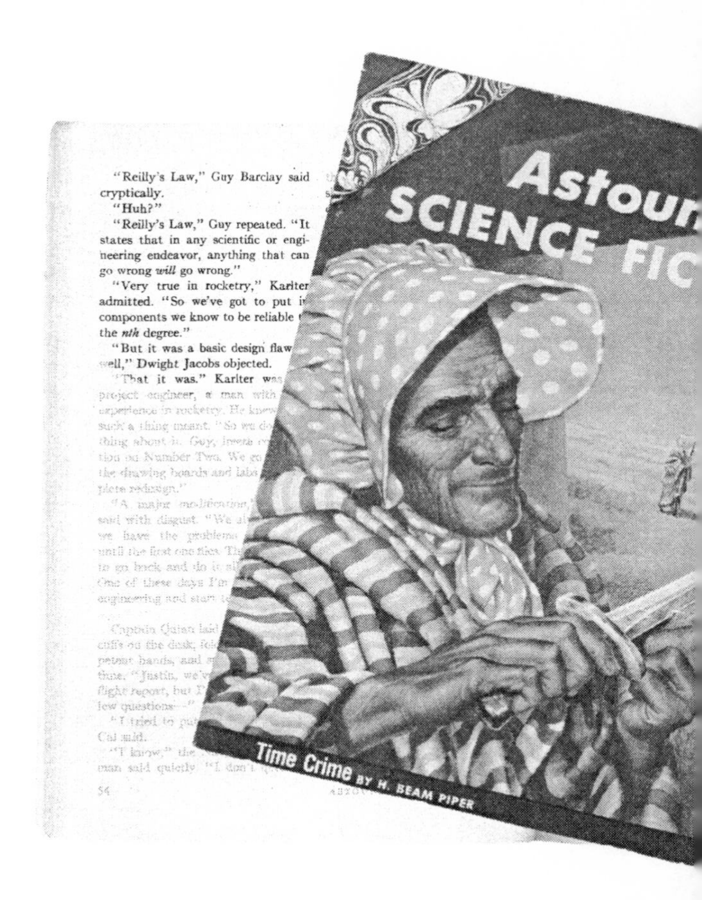
"Reilly's Law," Guy Barclay said cryptically.

"Huh?"

"Reilly's Law," Guy repeated. "It states that in any scientific or engineering endeavor, anything that can go wrong *will* go wrong."

"Very true in rocketry," Karlter admitted. "So we've got to put in components we know to be reliable to the *nth* degree."

"But it was a basic design flaw as well," Dwight Jacobs objected.

"That it was." Karlter was

Google. That's when I had what I felt might be, a major breakthrough. It turns out Lee Correy is a pseudonym for a prolific science and technical writer, now deceased, named G. Harry Stine. Stine was also an engineer who worked at White Sands in the 50's. Later in life he wrote the *Handbook of Model Rocketry*, something of a bestseller among hobbyists.

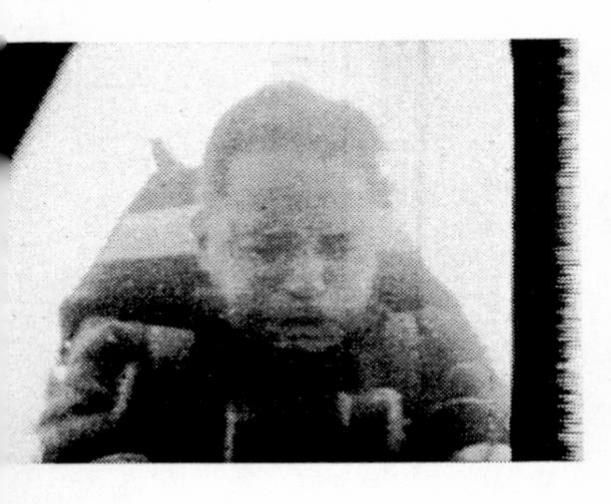

Connecting the dots... Considering that Holloman and White Sands are both located near Alamogordo, New Mexico, it certainly seems possible that Stine learned about the Law from Stapp, Murphy (who also lived in Alamogordo for a short time in the early 1950's) or one of their cohorts. As I noted in an email I wrote to Shapiro concerning the discovery, it seems an awfully strange co-incidence that the first reference in print to something resembling Murphy's Law was written by an author who lived in close proximity to two of the major players in the "classic" Murphy's Law origin story, during the same period.

On the heels of this I came to another realization. One thing that always bothered me was the fact that none of the newspaper or magazine articles I'd read concerning the rocket sled tests at Edwards ever mentioned Murphy's Law. Yet David Hill, George Nichols and others always pointed to a John Stapp press conference - some time after Ed Murphy made his infamous visit - as the key moment when Murphy's Law was revealed to an

The remains of the Gee Whiz track at Edwards' North Base. While much of the track has receded into the desert, a surprising amount of it remains. Here part of the emergency braking system — which consisted of a set of surplus aircraft wheels and a metal cable to catch a runway sled — sits forlornly in the grass. Photo by the Author.

unenlightened world. Looking back on my notes, I realized no one ever specifically stated the press conference took place at Edwards or gave a time frame for it. Perhaps then it actually took place at Holloman, years later. That kind of scenario made even more sense when I remembered Robert Murphy mentioned that Stapp lived in his family's neighborhood at Holloman. If that was the case, if Stapp saw Murphy almost every week, the Law could certainly have been on his mind and the tip of his tongue…

I sent Fred Shapiro a brief, exultant email. By this time I'd been out of touch with him for nearly two years. In the meantime his own research had taken a series of unexpected turns. He'd managed to find, he told me in his reply, a reference that eclipsed the one in "Design Flaw" in terms of import. A book entitled *Men, Rockets and Space Rats* published in 1955 contains this line: "Colonel Stapp's favorite takeoff on sober scientific laws — Murphy's Law, Stapp calls it —'Everything that can possibly go wrong will go wrong'."

Yet despite this and my own discovery concerning the Harry Stine connection, Shapiro remained deeply skeptical. "I believe," he wrote, "That the whole Edwards AFB story is suspect, since there is no shred of evidence for it prior to 1955. I also believe that Murphy's Law was an old proverb in many fields prior to any aviation connection." He noted that he'd found several references to Murphy's Law "as being an old theatrical maxim", and had

The brake stand area, about 2/3rds of the way down the track, as it appears today. While once history was made on this desolate stretch of desert, and rockets roared and brakes screamed, all here is now properly quiet. Photo by the Author.

located a 1952 mountain climbing book by legendary journalist John Sack entitled *The Butcher: The Ascent of Yerupaja* which contained the proverb "Anything That Can Possibly Go Wrong Does". He'd also stumbled across a 1941 statement "by a literary figure" whom he was not yet at liberty to name, that is "very similar to Murphy's Law."

And so it goes. I have to say that despite Shapiro's discoveries, I'm still of the opinion that the Law originated at Edwards with the MX981 team, and was named after Edward A. Murphy. Sure, something similar might have been coined by someone else: human beings have probably understood, appreciated and expressed the thought embodied by the Law since they developed tools back in the Paleolithic era. But it is Edward A. Murphy's Law which is the one that is justly famous, and the one that is cited whenever things go wrong.

Of course, at this point, I can't claim that I'm not biased. Sure, the possibility does exist that the whole story really is bunk. But that would mean that the various overlapping accounts as told by David Hill, George Nichols and Ed Murphy over the years are fiction. Furthermore it would mean that the bitter feud that raged between Nichols and Murphy for all those years was completely, utterly, ridiculously absurd - an argument over nothing. Ironically it would also render Nichols' and the second generation of Murphys' anger at me moot, while at the same time reducing my research to. . . nothing more than a futile, misguided, and entirely pointless endeavor.

Alas, I doubt we'll ever know one way or another, unless Shapiro or someone else out there finds a "smoking gun" document. Even then I'm confident some skeptic would dismiss it, debunk it or present a new theory. Given that, perhaps we shouldn't worry about knowing definitively where it came from, who first uttered it, and what exactly they said.

After all, I think we all have better things to do with our lives.

Col. John Paul Stapp received the Legion of Merit, and was elected to the National Aviation Hall of Fame and the Space Hall of Fame before he passed away in 1999. The "Stapp Car Crash Conference", an annual meeting of researchers and safety engineers, continues to this day and is now in its 50th year.

After fighting Parkinson's disease for many years, David Hill Sr. died in 2004. He never did make any further comments about Area 51.

Edward A. Murphy Jr. spent a long career working as a reliability engineer and died of natural causes in 1990.

George Nichols worked as a project manager for Northrop and at the Jet Propulsion Laboratory before retiring. He now lives quietly at his home near Los Angeles.

Dr. John Paul Stapp didn't risk his life for nothing. As a direct result of his research and lobbying, automobiles became safer. Many others made major contributions to this cause including the "Father of the Seatbelt" Dr. Hugh DeHaven, Volvo engineer Nils Bohlin who invented the three point restraint, and consumer advocate Ralph Nader who lobbied for federal auto safety standards.

The photos below dramatically illustrate several decades of progress. On the left, a 1964 Corvette Stingray features an unforgiving all-steel body that subjects occupants to terrific forces in a crash. The car originally came without seatbelts, although a two-piece "lap belt" could be purchased as an option. Notice the array of attractive, yet potentially injurious interior furnishings including a rather solid metal dashboard. Decelerating passengers who hit the dash could also impact hard plastic or solid metal projecting buttons, studs and dials. In a 1954 accident, for instance, entertainer Sammy Davis Jr. lost his eye to a decorative logo on the center of his Cadillac's steering wheel. The steel shaft of the steering assembly in the 'vette and many other cars built in this era also had a tendency to telescope, spearing drivers (such as the actor James Dean) involved in head-on collisions. Note the protruding metal door and window handles, and the glare-producing metal trim

Photos courtesy of Mike Machat, Wings and Airpower Magazine.

used on the dash, window frames and even the windshield wipers. The windshield on this car is likely laminated. While safer than other forms of glass, drivers and passengers who impacted it often received severe concussions and facial lacerations.

The late model Acura seen on the right, on the other hand, offers impact-reducing "crumple zones" and features an engine designed to drop to the ground in the event of a head-on crash. The interior is made of impact-absorbing plastics, controls are recessed, and the entire dash is padded. Matte and glare-resistant materials lessen distraction on the driver, while a host of other systems including safety glass, a breakaway steering wheel, three-point automatic seatbelts and airbags offer a much better chance for survival in a high-speed accident.

Despite these innovations people are killed in automobile accidents each and every day. Only 79% of Americans wear seatbelts, a rather disturbing statistic when you consider that "whatever can go wrong..." You might think about that next time you get in a car. Buckle up in memory of Dr. John Paul Stapp, and in *defiance* of Murphy's Law.

ABOUT THE AUTHOR

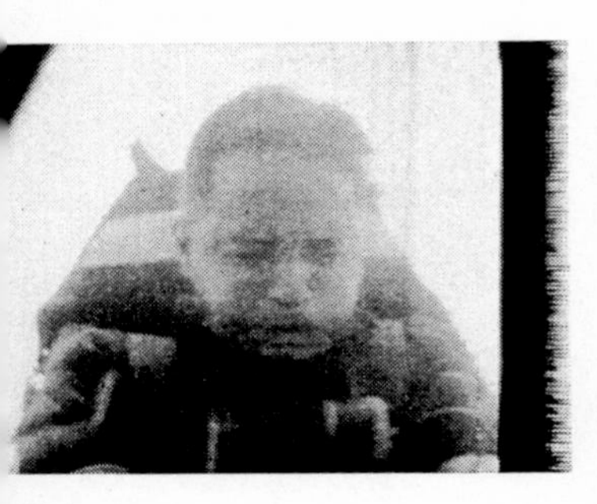

An award-winning writer and documentary filmmaker with a keen interest in aviation history, Nick T. Spark holds an M.F.A. in film production from the University of Southern California. He is a frequent contributor to history magazines including *Wings, Airpower, Naval History*, and the *Journal of the American Aviation Historical Society*. His documentary film *Regulus: The First Nuclear Missile Submarines* is currently airing on Discovery Channel Europe. He lives in Los Angeles where, whenever possible, he applies the lesson of preparedness imparted by "the Law". His garage is well stocked with earthquake survival supplies, he always wears his seatbelt, and he gets a medical check-up at least once a year. He likes to point out that all it takes to avoid many of the inevitable disasters that life throws our way, is a little forethought. As a result, prior to being published, the text and layout of this book was frequently backed up on several different computers and emailed to the far reaches of the globe, just "in case".

Transducer.

To demonstrate the forces the Gee Whiz produced, an experiment was conducted with the dummy "Oscar Eightball". The front of the Whiz was covered with planks, and the dummy secured with a thin belt. When the sled decelerated, Oscar became airborne so quickly that, as Dr. Stapp later recounted, "he left his rubber face behind." The hapless mannequin shot through the planks, landing in a forlorn heap. Fortunately for Stapp, who was no dummy, this test was never repeated, intentionally or accidentally, with a human subject.